MW01026554

LEAVING
101

How to Prepare to Leave Your
Alcoholic Husband —
Even If You're Not Ready to Leave Your
Alcoholic Husband

BY WREN WATERS

Also by Wren Waters:

THE ALCOHOLIC HUSBAND PRIMER:
Survival Lessons for the Alcoholics's Wife

SO YOU WANT TO WIN HER BACK:
Tough-Love Advice For The Alcoholic Who Wants To Save His Marriage

DO YOU KNOW I CRY DURING YOGA?
Letters From A Wife Who's Leaving

CONTENTS

Preface .... **vii**

Introduction .... **ix**

Part I: The Alcoholic Husband **1**

#1 Don't Prepare to Leave — Prepare to Have *the Choice* to Leave 3

#2 Give Yourself Permission to Leave 11

#3 Ignore the Loop 15

#4 Accept the Marriage You Have 21

#5 Grieve the Marriage You Don't Have 27

#6 Forgive Your Husband 31

#7 Re-Frame How You View Your Husband 35

#8 Prepare for the Guilt 39

#9 Accept That Your Husband Is an Alcoholic — and Then Let It Go 43

Part II: The Metaphysical (aka Lessons from a Lost Cat) **49**

#1 Believe in Something 51

#2 Lessons from a Lost Cat 55

#3 Choose a Different Way of Being in the Universe 67

#4 Ask the Universe for a Money-Reality Shift 73

#5 Learn from the Rice and Water 79

#6 Align Yourself with a Higher Power 85

#7 Move toward the Positive — Not Away from the Negative 89

Part III: Creating Order (among the Ordered Chaos of Your Life) **91**

#1 Defining Ordered Chaos 93

#2 Start by Getting Up in the Morning 95

#3 Start a Meditation Practice..101
#4 De-Clutter — Kinda!..105

Part IV: The Movement Requirement..**109**
#1 Decide What You Want Your Life to Be..111
#2 So Who Do You Want to Be?..115
#3 Don't Focus on Money..119
#4 The Movement Requirement..123
#5 Focus..131

Part VI: Living Your Life..**135**
#1 Life Your Life Where It Is..137
#2 Trust the Process..145
#3 This S**t Is Hard..149
#4 Change Your Internal Dialogue..153
#5 It's All a Head Game..157

And Finally... Consider the Gift of Alcoholism..**161**

Resources..**165**

Contact..**170**

Preface

There's not much worse for a writer than editing her book.

If writing is riding a horse as it gallops effortlessly across the open plain with the wind racing through your hair and a fresh breeze at your back, editing is mucking out the manure in the horse's stall and hauling around bales of straw for bedding. Editing is the part of being a writer that is not really about writing. It's agonizing over punctuation and paragraph breaks, doubting passages you once loved and questioning everything you have already put out to the world.

And yet it must be done.

Especially in this new world of self-publishing.

I knew so little about self-publishing when I began self publishing and the early editions of my books show it. Most of my first-edition books are downright embarrassing. And yet, I want to tell you I am happy I did it. I started. I got something out there. Even if it was incredibly amateurish.

Little will shackle you to the ground like life with an alcoholic husband. It steals your minutes, your hours, your days until one day you realize it has stolen years.

The years of your life.

It's taken me over 20 years to free myself emotionally so that I might free myself financially, mentally, spiritually and physically from the chains of an alcoholic marriage. I often chastise myself for not doing something "sooner." But it's hard to repair your boat when you are already sinking at sea.

And yet repair we must.

I see now that though my first books were sloppy and haphazard in terms of publishing standards, they were at least *something*. Some duct tape and wads of newspaper where water was rushing in and threatening to sink my life.

This book isn't so much about leaving the sinking ship that is your alcoholic marriage as it is about preemptively preparing the boat of your life for the storm. You may be experiencing the full force of that storm now or you may be feeling only the first raindrops and gusts of wind. But believe me, if you're married to an alcoholic, this storm is headed for you.

The alcoholic does not spontaneously get better.

In fact, alcoholism is a progressive disease and so the alcoholic who is not seeking sobriety is, by default, falling further into the abysses of his compulsive drinking. And whether you have been married for five years or ten, 20 years or more, it's never too late to rescue your life.

Or too early to start.

INTRODUCTION

Start before you are ready.
Steven Pressfield, Do The Work

I am married to an alcoholic.

As much as I hate the fact that this defines me, it defines me.

It inhabits my psyche and my soul and is present, to some degree, in my every single thought of my every single minute of my every single day.

I am never NOT aware of the fact that I am married to an alcoholic.

And I am never NOT aware of The Big Question looming over me: Should I stay or should I go?

No one thinks about leaving the alcoholic husband more than the wife of the alcoholic.

And yet people on the outside seem to think the idea alludes us.

They offer sage advice like "leave the bastard," throw the bum out" and "kick his ass to the curb" as if such thoughts never occurred to us.

Oh, they occur to us.

They occur to us...

All.

The.

Time.

But other thoughts occur to us as well.

Occupy our minds.

Haunt and taunt us day after day.

Like the bastard everyone wants us to leave...

The bum they all say we should kick out...

The ass (hole) well meaning friends and loved ones advocate we "kick to the curb..."

Is also the man we fell in love with.

The father of our children.

The one who held us when our father died or sat with us as our mother was diagnosed with cancer or got in the car in the middle of pouring rain and thundering lightening to look for the family dog.

That bastard, that bum, that asshole was the man we vowed to love and honor.

Til death do us part.

That bastard, that bum, that asshole is the one person we thought we could always count on. The one who was always going to have our back. The one we were to grow old and die with.

That bastard, that bum, that asshole is our past, our present and was suppose to be our future.

And so the question of whether to stay or go is not a stagnant one.

The question of whether to stay or go is a fluid question.

With an equally fluid, painfully oscillating answer.

PART I

The Alcoholic Husband

Alcoholics don't deny they're using.
They deny it's hurting others.
(SoberServices on Pinterest)

LESSON #1

Don't Prepare to Leave —
Prepare to Have *the Choice* to Leave

Destiny is not a matter of chance. It's a matter of choice.
It's not a thing to be waited for, it's a thing to be achieved.
William Jennings Bryan

I know the tape you have looping in your head.

I had the same tape looping in my own head for at least the last ten years of my 20+ years marriage.

I've got to leave.

I need to stay.

I can't take this.

I'm leaving him!

What about my vows?

How can I live like this another minute longer?

I can do this for my family.

I!

HAVE GOT!

TO!

GET OUT!!!!

It's ok. I'll make it work.

I'm going to stay.

NOOOOOOOOOOO!! I can't! I JUST! Can't!

Women don't stay with their alcoholic husbands because they never decide to leave.

Women stay with their alcoholic husbands because they decide to leave... over and over and over again.

I don't believe a woman can stayed married to an alcoholic *and* be the very best version of herself and live her life to its greatest potential. It's a hard, even controversial, stance to take. I know that. And for those who disagree, I don't disagree with you. The waters of an alcoholic marriage are known waters and yet uncharted waters. Each must chart her own course, set her own sexton and sail her own journey. If a woman tells me she is happy and content and has found the way to her best possible life and version of herself all while staying in an alcoholic marriage, it is not for me to debate or put her on the defensive.

But I've been doing this married-to-an-alcoholic thing for a long time now. I've been a witness to my own tragic transformation from a rather positive, upbeat and passionate individual, excited about life and my place in it into an angry, hostile, raging wreck of a human. I've dragged myself through the days as all I once knew, valued and loved within myself drained from me like beer flowing from a tap. I've woken up to my soul feeling as vacant and empty as the beer cans that littered my kitchen counter.

And I've listened to many other women, wives of alcoholics such as myself, as they've recounted the loss of their being and all they once held dear. I've cried my own tears, held others as they cried theirs, as the far-reaching claw of the Beast of Alcoholism destroyed families, dreams and futures.

It really is *this bad* being married to an alcoholic.

I know there are women who debate, disagree and even denounce my stance. But I also know there are other women — far too many other women — who fear the brokenness that awaits them if they don't do something. For myself, it eventually came down to one of only two choices:

Leave and survive.

Or,

Stay and die.

Being married to an alcoholic may not kill you physically —
though there is certainly tragic potential for life-threatening illnesses
due to the long-term stress of living with a compulsive drinker — but
it will kill you emotionally, spiritually and mentally.

And yet, I know statistically most women do not leave their
alcoholic husbands.

*It took me over 20 years to firmly and completely solidify my own desire
and willingness to leave my alcoholic husband.*

I wanted to leave him.

Except when I didn't.

I knew I had to.

Except when I thought I could stay.

I made plans on how to leave.

Except I never followed through on any of them.

It put me a difficult place as a writer.

I wanted to write a book about how to leave your alcoholic
husband.

Except I didn't know how to leave my own alcoholic husband.

"How are you going to write about leaving your alcoholic husband
if you can't leave your alcoholic husband," the critic in me taunted.

"How can you be genuine?" It chided.

"How would such a book even have any sort of conviction and
sincerity," It demanded to know.

"Who," It went for my writer's jugular vein, "writes a self-help
book when she can't even help herself?"

Of course I had no reasonable answer for my inner critic because
the truth was, I couldn't advise other women on what to do or how
to do it when I couldn't do it myself. I couldn't write a book about
leaving an alcoholic marriage when my own two feet were planted,
albeit it with delicate, vulnerable roots, in the toxic rich soil of my own
alcoholic marriage.

And then one day I was talking to a woman who had been married
to her alcoholic husband for more than 30 years.

She was tired.

So very, very tired.

I was trying to be positive and encouraging. I told her it wasn't "too late." I asked her what her dreams had been when she was younger. I tried to coax her into fantasizing about her ideal life. She wasn't indifferent to my efforts but she looked at me, and with the saddest, emptiest eyes I've ever seen, said,

"Thank you Wren but I don't care anymore. Not about him. Not about his drinking. Not about me. Not about my life. I. Just. Don't. Care. Anymore."

And I knew she meant it.

She didn't care.

Worse.

She didn't care that she didn't care.

And that's when the tragic paradox of the alcoholic marriage came to me:

When a woman knows she needs to leave...

When she still has the emotional and mental strength to walk out the door and start a new life...

When she still has a proper perspective on the toxicity of an alcoholic husband...

When there is still enough of her, enough of her heart and soul left, to leave...

She doesn't necessarily want to leave.

She still feels she can handle the marriage on a daily basis.

She still enjoys (even if they are fleeting and diminishing) moments of love and warmth with her husband.

She still feels a sense of control over herself and her life.

The knocks come.

The days that drop her to her knees.

The incidences that seem to eviscerate her internal organs.

They are there.

They are happening.

She is doing the dance trying to manage her alcoholic husband's behavior, keep her children safe and protect her own soul — all that is most certainly happening.

But there is still a strength to her.

A willingness.

A determination.

She believes she can hold onto herself, protect her family, live her best life and still honor her wedding vows.

But alcoholism is a cruel, brutal and relentless foe.

It gets the alcoholic, it gets the alcoholic's wife and it gets everyone around the alcoholic, in the clenches of its nasty, foul claws and it rips and shreds, tears and slices til there is nothing left but the bloody fibers of your being.

And now you know you want to leave.

Now you must leave.

But there's nothing left in you to leave with.

Emotionally, spiritually, mentally you are tatters.

Nothing but strands of sinew where a whole being once existed.

And now what do you do as you will yourself to move but watch helplessly as the Beast sucks the last bit of marrow from your being?

It's scary to make the decision to leave.

In fact, for most of us, it will prove too scary.

As the wives of alcoholics we experience so many varied, contradictory and conflicting emotions regarding our husbands and marriages that it's little wonder we repeatedly get tripped up in our efforts to leave. (Or stay.) One day we feel as though we can't possible endure *another single second* in our situation...

But then he's reading to our kids or fixing the hot water heater or helping out in some other manner and we think,

"Well maybe..."

One weekend he is passed out on what could be a beautiful Sunday afternoon and all you can feel is disgust and disdain as you look at him...

But then the next weekend you're all together on a family outing
and it seems your heart pauses and says,

"Well maybe..."

The alcoholic marriage is tragically deceitful because all things
are not all bad all at once. It's far more insidious and gradual than
that. Like emptying the ocean with a teaspoon. Except one day the
teaspoon becomes a tablespoon. Then the tablespoon becomes a
cup. The cup a bucket. Until one day the impossible happens and the
bottom of the seemingly bottomless ocean is revealed.

Drip, drip, drip go the waters of your marriage, your soul, your being.
You hardly notice at first.

Until one day, all at once but over the course of many, many years,
behind your back but right before your eyes, every ounce of life has
been drained out of your marriage, your soul, your very being.

So what is the solution?

How can a woman prepare to leave her alcoholic husband when
she can't fully committed to leaving her alcoholic husband? What
can (should?) a woman do when her life feels like a daily exercise in
processing and managing conflicting emotions? What is the solution
when the words in her head and the feelings in her heart seem
mutually exclusive? I spent (wasted?) so many years of my life in an
emotional limbo because I thought I needed a definitive answer to the
"leave or go question" before I took action. I now see it was foolish
to ever expect that I would one day arrive at an unequivocal, "Yes,
I'm leaving" or "No, I'm staying" state of being. The place a woman
occupies emotionally, mentally and even spiritually within the
alcoholic marriage is too volatile, too tentative and mercurial for her
to wait for an unwavering conviction — in either direction — before
she takes action in defense of her own life and the future she wants
for herself.

The answer is so painfully obvious that it can hide in plain sight:
Don't prepare to leave.
Prepare to have *the choice* to leave.

Stop thinking about whether you should leave or stay.

Stop "deciding" one way or another.

Do not entertain the Big L question a second longer.

In fact, you don't even need to *want* to leave.

You just need (and hopefully want) to have the desire to one day have *the choice* as to whether you leave or stay.

As they say, no one can predict the future.

(They also say past behavior is the greatest predictor of future behavior but we'll leave that alone for now as far as the alcoholic husband's trajectory is concerned.)

There are certain things that can be predicted with considerable accuracy and one of them is this:

If you work hard to create a life for yourself that gives you the *option* to leave but never actually leave, or ever even want to leave, you won't regret the changes you created within yourself and for your life.

But, if you don't work hard to create a life that gives you the option to leave and then one day, five or ten or 15 years from now, *wish desperately for that option,* you will regret it tremendously.

So make the decision now that your goal is to work to take back control of your life. Your focus is not on leaving your marriage; your focus is on creating a life that gives you *the option* — mentally, emotionally, physically, spiritually and financially — *to leave.*

LESSON #2

Give Yourself Permission to Leave

I didn't leave because I stopped loving you.
I left because the longer I stayed, the less I loved myself.
Rupi Kaur

I know!

I just said don't think in terms of preparing to leave your husband; think in terms of preparing to have the choice to leave your husband. But now I'm saying give yourself permission to leave.

Huh?

No, I am not saying two contradictory things.

You do want to think in terms of creating a life that allows you the choice to leave — whether that decision comes today, tomorrow, ten years from now or never at all.

But you still need to give yourself permission to leave.

Imagine your child didn't know for sure if she wanted to go to college. You would probably tell her to work hard in high school so that when the day comes, it will be her *choice* as to whether or not she goes to college. But you wouldn't say,

"Work hard so you have the choice. But I'm not going to *let* you go to college no matter what you decide when the time comes."

You could have the self discipline of a Tibitan guru, the focus of a Buddhist monk and the determination of an Olympic athlete and you still wouldn't work toward something you would never be allowed to achieve.

Leaving your alcoholic marriage is such a big head game. In fact, I suspect it is far, far bigger than you realize at the moment. I know for me it was.

All I wanted — and I mean *All! I! WANTED!!* for years was to buy my own house and leave my alcoholic husband and marriage behind. I mean, I wanted this so badly that I could feel a true physical sensation, aching almost, within myself when I would drive around and look at houses and dream.

I wanted my own house SO! God DAMN! BAD!!

I thought that was enough.

In fact, I thought that was all that matter.

I just needed to *want* it.

And yet, as the necessary players began lining up (i.e. my finances) and I began to know that indeed, this was going to happen for me, waves of nausea and anxiety would periodically flash through me. At first, I attributed this to my being nervous at the thought of telling my husband and my children but deep down I knew it wasn't about them at all. I knew it was really about me and my life and this huge *accomplishment* I was allowing myself to bring forward. I've long known I suffer from not a fear of failure but a fear of success and you don't get much more successful than buying your dream house. It scared me.

It really, really, really scared me.

Maybe that's why it took me ten years to get there. If not for the work I had done within myself, I suspect that this fear would have brought about some sort of internal sabotage. I don't know if you have a fear of success, as I did. Maybe a fear of failure. Maybe you've never been allowed or encouraged to see yourself as a competent woman who has not just the ability but also the right to create the life of her dreams. Whatever demons or ghosts may haunt you, begin their exorcism by giving yourself permission to leave your marriage one day, should you so desire.

It doesn't mean you have to leave.

It doesn't mean you will leave.

But it does mean that you will allow yourself to create and live a life that will give you that option. It does mean you will allow yourself that choice should you ever come to deem it necessary.

LESSON #3

Ignore the Loop

We cannot solve our problems with the same thinking we used when we created them.
Albert Einstein

First, before I talk about The Loop, let me say in regards to the above quote, I do not believe that as the wife of an alcoholic, you created the problems of living with an alcoholic. The alcoholic creates the problems in the alcoholic household. However, since you are the one who hopes to fix and save her own life, you are the one who will benefit from recognizing that you may now be locked into a certain way of thinking. No doubt the result of living with a compulsive drinker and all the associated toxicity and turmoil but locked into a pattern of thinking none the less. And so if you want to save and change your life, you need to challenge, change, shake up your way of thinking.

For myself, I came to recognize this way of thinking as The Loop.

The Loop is what will keep you shackled in your alcoholic marriage.

The Loop is what will contribute to the gradual, insidious but eventual erosion of your life.

The Loop is what steals the days of you life — one second at a time. It's what eats your souls, one bite at a time.

What is The Loop?

You may have never considered it by this name.

In fact, you may have never actually identified it within yourself or been consciously aware of it.

But it's there.

You've heard it.

Felt it.

Experience the destruction of your life at its hands.

The Loop is that constant barrage of conflicting emotions I've already mentioned.

The opposing thoughts that filter in and out of your mind on a daily basis

I'M LEAVING!

I need to stay.

Oh God! I can't stand this a MINUTE longer!

I took a vow.

I HATE HIM!

I still love him.

I can't live like this!

The kids want their dad.

Blah, blah, blah.

Etc., etc., etc...

And so and so forth.

These conflicting feelings and thoughts don't exist because you are "co-dependent."

They don't stem from the erroneous notion that you are the "enabler" to your husband's addiction.

And lord knows their genesis didn't take root in some bizarre satisfaction you experience by living in an alcoholic household with an alcoholic husband.

No, these paradoxical and contradictory feelings are the direct result of being human.

A loving, caring, nurturing human to be exact. Who is often at the mercy of her own emotions.

We love to think of emotions as either/or. Black or white. Right or wrong. Good or bad. But your emotions aren't individual necklaces hanging neatly from a jewelry organizer. No, your emotions are that ball of chains at the bottom of you jewelry box. The silver tangled up with the gold. The expensive intertwined with the costume. Long chains, short chains all knotted together.

That's your emotions.

Knotted and tangled and intertwined.

Further complicating your emotions is your husband.

He is not a non-entity or neutral contributor to your confusing and conflicted feelings.

Even if there is drinking from the very first day of a marriage, as there was in mine, the alcoholic marriage doesn't start out *bad*.

It starts out good.

Loving and intimate, connected and caring.

Then something not so good happens.

A drunken night.

An ugly outburst.

But then things are good again.

Then a little more bad.

Then it's good — good — bad.

Then maybe good — bad — good.

Until one day it's more bad then good but it doesn't happen all at once or in a definitive manner. It's slow. It's gradual. It's deceiving. It's corrosive and erosive. For certain, one day it becomes just all bad but it's never all bad, all at once. If it was, if your marriage to an alcoholic was *always ba*d, your brains would be better suited at getting you out.

The human brain is designed to move away from what hurts or makes it feel bad and move toward, want more of, what feels good or is pleasurable. So what happens when the human brain is trying to process a constant barrage of conflicting emotions?

A lot of mental chaos and indecision.

Studies have been done where they condition two groups of test-critters (not sure the species, probably monkeys) to push a lever in order to receive a treat/reward. One group receives the treat/reward *every single time* the lever is pushed. The other group receives their treat/reward randomly. Sometimes one push of the lever, sometimes two or three, maybe four or more frustrating pushes of that lever before a tasty morsel pops out.

Once the researchers had adequately conditioned both groups to expect their reward for the arduous task of pushing a lever, you know what they did?

Yep, they took the treat-reward *away!* (Researchers are like that.)

And what they found was... drum roll please.

The group of trusting little critters who always got their reward after just one push, *abandoned their efforts sooner* than the group who was conditioned to expect a reward sporadically and randomly.

It makes sense of course.

The random group was lead to believe if it just pushed that damn lever long enough, eventually that little hunk of barely nothing at all would come tumbling out.

What happens to you on a mental and emotional level when married to an alcoholic is similar to this.

You become conditioned to just wait it out.

Your thoughts and emotions may be doing somersaults in your head, but you, yourself are just waiting.

And pushing the lever.

Dinner, kids, laundry. Work, dog to the vet, kids to the doctor. Soccer, ballet, parent-teacher conferences. You just keep doing what you have to do, asking yourself should you stay, telling yourself you need to leave, assuring yourself you want to stay, making life work for you and your family the best you can.

You have to learn to ignore The Loop.

You have to decide the question of staying or leaving is not the question right now.

Thoughts and ideas gain power because we give them our attention.

Practice not "hearing" The Loop or responding to it but also, don't try to shut it down. You know the adage about the kid who is acting up: "any attention is good attention. Any engagement with these thoughts — even the denouncement of them — is engagement that keeps them alive. You're going for zero engagement. Like ignoring the kid sliding around on his belly as you try to talk to the air condition repair man.

Remember, your goal isn't preparing to leave your alcoholic husband anyway; your goal is preparing to *have the choice to leave*. You don't have to answer, decide or dwell on the question of should you or shouldn't you leave. You don't have to allow yourself to be jerked around emotionally as The Loop threatens to high-jack your thinking and your efforts! Let the chatter of The Loop be nothing more than background noise that you don't respond to in any way. Like the kid sliding around on his belly, sooner or later both get tired out.

LESSON #4

Accept the Marriage You Have

Alcoholics make very poor husbands.
Anonymous

Raise your hand if your picture of happily-ever-after included an alcoholic husband.

If, as you walked down the aisle or popped into the court house, you dreamed of one day being told to shut the fuck up and/or being called a fucking bitch.

Raise you hand if among the images of chubby babies and family vacations, you also pictured beer bottles littering your home, liquor bottles stashed in their not-too-hiding hiding places.

Say "me, me, me" if you expected to lay down on many a night, too many a nights, next to a passed out husband.

Or if you were looking forward to a husband who wanted sex though he was barely sober enough to walk.

Say "yes" if your understanding of the "worse" in the "for better or worse" of your vows meant family vacations and holidays hijacked by your husband's drunken behavior or repeated calls to "come get me" because he was once again too drunk to drive or countless DUI's piling up like dirty laundry in a teenager's room.

Nod your head in the affirmative if you expected, on any level, that the backdrop of your marriage, your home and your life would be one of an emotional and metal toxicity with such intensity and so prevailing that you watched your own sense of being erode and disappear. To be replaced with anger, regret and hopelessness.

No one sets out to marry an alcoholic.

No one chooses voluntarily to live with a man who will curse her.
Belittle her.

Call her names.

Ignore her needs or demand his needs always be placed above
hers and everyone else's in the household.

No woman purposely agrees to partner with a man who will be
emotionally vacant.

Or will turn her life into a game of mental hopscotch where all she
can do is jump from square to square, hoping to maintain her balance
and survive each landing.

The conditions and experiences, undertones and daily reality
of living with an active alcoholic just aren't a part of any woman's
dreams and plans for her life and future as she says,

"I do."

The majority of women, like me, like you, who marry alcoholics
first marry a man we are in love with. A man we find charming and
loving, hard working and kind. Fun and great in bed. We marry a man
we laugh with, cry with (not *because of*), tell the secrets of our soul to
and listen to his secrets. We marry a man we want to spend the rest of
our lives with.

We, sadly and tragically, just don't realize that we are not seeing
the full picture.

That along with the charming and caring, hard working and sexy,
is a beast. The Beast of Alcoholism.

Compulsive drinking changes a man.

It's that simple.

It takes the man who seemed so warm, so kind, so easy to love
and be loved by and changes him profoundly. For me, my charming,
loving, fun and fun-in-bed, etc. man became a selfish, self absorbed,
verbally abusive, emotionally absent, husband. Your husband may
be just like that, kind a like that, not like that or not like that yet. But
one thing is absolutely certain: if your husband is an alcoholic, it will

change him. And not in any way that is even remotely good or that you can like.

The problem is the Beast of Alcoholism is not only cruel but cunning and quite insidious as well. The changes are gradual, but explosive. All at once but then receding. Daily but then in remission. The man you love, but who is an alcoholic, is not going to suddenly be this drunken bastard *one day*. No, the man you love will be there, then disappear, then be back, only to disappear again. But then be back. Temporarily. It's a systematic destruction that interferes with your own judgment and confuses your emotionally. It makes it difficult to maintain perspective not just on your marriage but on your husband and yourself as well.

But here's the basic (sad) truth:

You are married to an alcoholic.

That's a hard, hard pill to swallow. Most of us spend years upon years spiting it out, only to try swallowing it again later. It's all part of the loop. Part of that continued hope that can eventually rob you of your sense of self and your life. The alcoholic marriage is:

Volatile.

Wanting.

Vacant.

Verbally abusive.

One sided.

Stressful.

Hurtful.

Mundane (at its best)

Taxing.

Difficult.

Painful.

And it just gets worse from there.

When you are married to an alcoholic, you live in an emotional dessert while allowing yourself to believe the once yearly rainfall will last.

You mistake the few drops of dew that appear in the early morning as an abundance of water.

You think the mirage of a glistening lake just off in the distance is real.

It's not something to blame or condemn yourself for.

Who wouldn't hold out hope that the drought that has become your marriage and your life is the facade while the sporadic (and ever diminishing) moments of tenderness, connection, love and joy is the truth?

But it's not.

You know that.

But you know what else?

Most marriages aren't what they seem to the outside world.

I spent so many years expecting my marriage should be a version of perfect, believing that most marriages are a version of perfect. But as I shared and was open about my own marriage, it seemed more women shared and were open about their own marriages. I'm not speaking only of alcoholic marriages. As a friend of mine put it in regards to her seemingly "perfect" marriage being exposed for what it really was — marriage to a man who was emotionally abusive and manipulative:

"People started coming out of the woodwork at church. Telling me how miserable they were. How they wished they had my courage to leave."

I don't say this as a cynic but rather only as a woman who's unhappy marriage caused even more unhappiness due to my own expectations that everyone else was in a happy, healthy marriage while I was slogging through the emotional tar pit mine had become. It was like I had seen a white tiger once in my life. And now was disappointed and angered when every tiger I was saw wasn't white. Of course, the majority of tigers are orange.

Marriages are mostly orange tigers.

I'm not trying to be disparaging about marriages. But I do believe when you stop expecting your marriage *should* be the white tiger of holy matrimony, it makes it a bit easier to accept it for the orange tiger it is.

It took me over ten years to accept my marriage for what it is. (I would highly recommend and encourage you to speed up the process if at all possible.) Much of this time was lost, no doubt, to the fact that I was expecting (requiring?) my marriage to look like a print add for Pottery Barn furniture or some random person's post on Instagram.

Advertising and social media are full of only white tigers. We know there are orange tigers. We know most tigers are orange. But after looking at picture after picture after picture, year after year after year, of white tigers, we forget. We begin to think all tigers are white.

You and me, we didn't get the white tiger of marriages.

Some people do.

(Most people don't.)

You and I certainly did not.

Why not?

Because we married alcoholics.

(Not only are out tigers orange, they are drunk as well.)

And why did we marry alcoholics?

Because we fell in love with men...

Who turned out to be alcoholics.

Not because we secretly wanted this pandemonium for our marriages; not because we are broken or defective; not because we thought we could fix him. We just fell in love with men who were the right-guy-at-the-time but turned out to be the wrong or not-so-right-guy in the long run.

But whether you stay in your marriage or you one day decide to leave it, your life doesn't have to be hopelessly shackled to the chaos your marriage is today. You don't need to be drug around like an unfortunate antelope in the jaws of a tiger.

You, me, everyone who has ever gotten married, all wanted a healthy, happy marriage.

And there's no doubt you tried.

For a long time.

But creating a successful marriage with an active alcoholic is about as easy and as effective as trying to paint an orange tiger white.

Even if you can get the paint on, it's not going to stick.

Let go of what your marriage isn't.

Accept what it is.

You just may find that you can be your own white tiger.

LESSON #5

Grieve the Marriage You Don't Have

I just feel pain. A lot of it.
I thought I could imagine how much this would hurt, but I was wrong.
Haruki Murakami

So exactly *how* do you accept what your marriage is?

How do you put those dreams of happily-ever-after *with your husband* to rest?

(Don't ever give up on your own happily-ever-after.)

First and foremost, acknowledge the very real loss that you are experiencing.

The outside world doesn't see your loss. In fact, the outside world pretty much denies the loss, sending the very clear message that if your husband is an alcoholic and you end the marriage, it's for the better.

You haven't lost *anything*!

You've gained.

Your life.

Your sanity.

Your freedom.

Maybe.

But you've lost something too.

If you have children, they have certainly lost something.

And yes, even your no-good-alcoholic-bum of a husband has lost something.

In accepting what your marriage is, you also have to accept what it isn't.

And there is a very real loss that comes with that. A loss you are going to have to acknowledge and experience and process.

When you are married to an alcoholic, you have lost the friend, the confidant, the buddy, the one-man fan club you were expecting in a husband. Who you had for a time.

You have lost the lover, (if not completely, you will most likely loss the attentive, loving-lover you once had), the supportive partner you thought you'd be sharing the trials and tribulations of life with, the co-parent you thought you'd be sharing the trials and tribulations of raising children with.

You have lost that person to whom you once laid next to in the middle of the night, dark and quiet settled over the world, and shared your biggest fears, your grandest wishes with.

You have lost the man you planned your retirement with, dreamed of chubby cheek grandbabies with, the man you imaged you would built a cabin in the woods with or renovate a cottage by the sea with.

Additionally, you don't just lose what you won't get.

You also lose what you can't give.

You have lost the spouse you long to be a friend *to*.

A husband for whom you can be his one-woman-fan club.

A man you can give hope to when he is feeling hopeless, make life's burdens a little lighter when they threaten to be break him.

The loss of giving is as real and poignant as the loss of receiving.

I remember I used to volunteer to do things for my husband. Or just do them without being asked.

I'd do his laundry. Fold it. Put it away.

I didn't mind.

If I did laundry late in the night, I'd lay a pair of clean socks and a towel in the bathroom for him so he didn't have to go searching in the basement the next morning, when he had to get up at 5 am to get ready for work.

Sometimes he'd realize at 9 or 10 at night he needed gas. My husband *hates* getting gas early in the morning before work. I'd volunteer to take his car out and fill it up that night.

I'm not offering these things as proof at how wonderful a wife I was.

I don't think what I did or offered was out of the ordinary.

That's what you do for each other when you are married.

Simple things.

Pain in the ass things.

Little things that make your spouse's life better in a big way.

But as my husband did less and less for me, I began to do less and less for him.

I was mad.

Resentful.

Screw him.

And in that I lost something.

I lost being able to fulfill in me the very real human need to give.

You lose so much (SO! MUCH!) when you are married to an alcoholic.

It's real loss.

Not just loss listed on a page in a book.

And you have the right to grieve this and in fact, you should grieve it.

Take the time to really notice and mourn all you have lost in your marriage.

Acknowledge the deep pain of not just all you relationship is, but also all that it isn't.

Feel it.

Allow it.

Validate it.

Grieve it.

So that you might move beyond it.

LESSON #6

Forgive Your Husband

When a deep injury is done to us, we never heal until we forgive.
Nelson Mandela

Your husband is an alcoholic.

Does that mean he's a calculating asshole who chooses beer or vodka or whiskey (or beer AND vodka AND whiskey) over you, your marriage and your family?

Your husband is an alcoholic.

Does that mean the selfishness within him is of such depth and magnitude that he doesn't care how much his drinking hurts you?

Your husband is an alcoholic.

Does that mean that he so loves the taste and high of his drink-of-choice that regardless of your feelings, your wishes and desires, he's going to drink anyway?

Or...

Your husband is an alcoholic.

Does it mean that he is a complete but unwilling victim of genetics?

Your husband is an alcoholic.

Does that mean he drew the short-genetic straw and is physiologically unable to resist the pull of alcoholic beverages?

Your husband is an alcoholic.

Does that mean that he suffers from a disease and just like anyone else with a disease, he should be extended sympathy, compassion and understanding?

Your husband is an alcoholic.

Is it his fault?

Or is he a victim?

Guess what?

It.

Doesn't.

Matter.

Victim or responsible? Disease or choice? The debate will rage on long past you, me, our (alcoholic) husbands and our marriages are still of this Earth.

You can say it is his fault.

You can say he is a victim.

At the end of the day, the results are the same. The affects on you and your marriage are the same.

So if you need to blame him. Blame him. If you need to absolve him of blame, absolve him of blame. Because it doesn't really matter. Because either way, here is what you have to do:

Forgive him.

Forgive him for being a drunk.

Forgive him for being selfish.

Forgive him for being verbally abusive. (Yes, forgive him for this.)

Forgive him for being physically present but emotionally absent from you and your marriage.

Forgive him for his inability to communicate.

Forgive him for his anger.

Forgive him for leaving the toilet seat up, the kitchen cabinet doors open and putting empty milk containers back into the refrigerator.

Forgive him for the man he is.

And the man he isn't.

Forgive him for dragging you and your relationship, your family and your life into the tar pit of alcoholism.

Forgive him every drunken holiday.

Every sleepless night.

Forgive every single wrong, every single wicked word, every

single way he has hurt you, disappointed you, let you down and/or abandoned you. Forgive him for yesterday; forgive him for today. Forgive him for tomorrow before tomorrow even happens.

Forgive him for being an alcoholic.

With every fiber of your being.

Forgive him.

Forgive him because to do less will only further your own destruction.

Resentment is corrosive.

Resentment is a cancer.

Resentment does the Beast's bidding.

It burrows into your soul.

And eats you from the inside out.

Forgive him for you.

LESSON #7

Re-Frame How You View Your Husband

If you change the way you look at things,
the things you look at change.
Wayne Dyer

This idea came to me spontaneously last year when we were on vacation at the beach.

As is true for most alcoholics, the worse comes out in my husband at the supposedly best times: vacations, holidays and in general, any moments of celebration and joy. Go figure? I have no idea why other than the alcohol may be flowing more freely at such times. I do know the "phenomena" tends to be rather universal among families with an active alcoholic. You want to enjoy the full brunt of an alcoholic's behavior — experience a holiday or vacation with him.

Last year as I was trying to enjoy the sun and surf but my husband was getting pissed off at the wind blowing over the umbrella, I thought,

"What if we were divorced and we were only vacationing together for the kids?

I then knew instantly that in that scenario, all (ALL!) the things he did that were so (SO!!) maddening, I would chalk up to "this is why we're divorced."

So now when we go anywhere — and we actually don't go places together as a family that often — but when we do and his driving is annoying me (and/or scaring me!) or his cursing is bad or he is just rather miserable to be around, I tell myself, "this is why we are divorced." It's not the best situation for all involved but it's better. Divorced couples will often revert back to their best behavior of when the relationship was fresh, young and respectful. I suppose in the early, idyllic days it's more out of a desire to impress rather than to avoid conflict but whatever can get you smoothly through a day is fair game, in my book. Viewing my husband as my *ex*-husband was surprisingly and refreshingly liberating. It brought me a depth of patience I couldn't have imagined or guessed at. To be clear, it didn't make his behavior *less* annoying, maddening or toxic but it did prevent his behavior from burrowing its ugly little self into the marrow of my soul.

At home I employ another mental trick.

I pretend that I am a single mother and my husband is "just" the boarder I rent a room to because I need the money!

I know!

Brilliant, right?

My mental scenario goes something like this:

I am a single, working mother. Money is tight for now. I rent a room to this "guy" and he does really annoying things like he doesn't clean up after himself, he leaves dishes in the sink and he drinks too much but he pays his rent on time. Most times he just hides away in his "rented" room, which is fine with me. He will help with some things if I ask. And most important, *I can TOTALLY trust him around my kids and possessions!!*

I mean, really, if you think about what you would want and need in a roommate should you have to rent out a room in your house, wouldn't it be a) pays rent on time and b) can totally trust him around your family and possessions? You would put up with the annoying, pain-in-the-ass stuff because the rent and trust are such HUGE issues!

So that's how I think of my husband.

When he leaves crap all over.

When he does nothing all week end.

When I'm doing laundry and cleaning the kitchen and doing all the yard work. Again.

He's a boarder who pays on time and whom I can trust.

It may sound silly.

It may seem unfair, exasperating or even infuriating that you have to create a fantasy (and not the fun kind!) in order to live with your husband. But living with an alcoholic is unfair, exasperating and infuriating too so which one would you prefer?

As far as feeling silly?

I've felt silly.

And I've felt my soul shriviling up and dying.

I'll take feeling silly any time.

LESSON #8

Prepare for the Guilt

Guilt is to the spirit what pain is to the body.
Elder David A Bednar

Of all the things that will derail you the surest and the quickest
in your effort to create financial, emotional, mental and spiritual
freedom for yourself, perhaps the most tenacious — and surprising —
will be guilt.

Guilt.

As in guilt over leaving your no-good, drunk-ass-bum, bastard of a
husband.

Guilt over leaving a man who sits in the basement drinking
himself into a stupor while you cook dinner, clean the kitchen, ferry
kids around town and feed the dog.

Guilt over someone who has, and will again, say the most vile,
ugly, viscous things to you.

Guilt over your husband who sleeps it off while you sit alone in the
dark, crying over all he, you, your life and marriage have become.

Yep, that guilt exactly.

"How, why the hell would I feel guilty?" You may be thinking.
"When I can finally leave, I am walking out and *never* looking back."

Yeah, maybe.

But probably not.

As ugly and nasty and debilitating and soul-sucking as living with
the alcoholic husband is, it's still not painless to end the marriage and
leave him.

You're leaving someone behind to die, if not literally certainly metaphorically. When I used to think of life without my husband, ironically what held me back was this:

I KNEW I could do it!

I knew I could build a life of my own, on my own, without him.

I also knew that he most likely would continue living-while-not-really-living just the way he was: go to work, come home, drink, wake up and repeat. In fact, I actually feared that if and when the kids and I were gone, his drinking would intensify and become worse. No matter how ugly and cruel your husband is to you and regardless of the degree to which he is checked out of the marriage and family life and in spite of the fact that he acts as though he wouldn't even notice if you walked out the door one day and never came back... you (and your children if you have them) are *the! Most! Important thing in the world to him!*

In fact, you're more than just important to him.

You are his life line.

Yes, his life line even though there may be days when treats you worse than a mangy stray dog on the street. Despite the fact that he holds you responsible for every single thing wrong in his life and never mind that he projects all his shortcomings onto you.

You're still his lifeline.

But you already knew this. Maybe not consciously. Maybe you think you didn't know but you knew. Deep in your heart. And so when you begin to actively work toward the possibility of, having the choice to, severing his life line — even though you know and believe and tell yourself it would be for the betterment of your family, guilt will come charging in like heavily armed storm troopers.

It's not because we're "enablers" or "co-dependent" or broken in some other way.

It's because we're caring, compassionate people. You and me.

It's part of what got us into this mess in the first place. The less caring, less compassionate, maybe even a little more selfish woman would have been gone long ago. But you and me? We don't know how to simply turn our backs on someone we love or even once loved. We can't will ourselves to ignore his potential suffering should we leave. "Abandonment" of others, even when it is necessary for our own survival, does not come natural or easy to us.

Just be prepared.

Know that this guilt is a natural part of the process.

It took me a *long* time to move past the guilt. I think in part because I kept trying to deny the guilt. How could I feel guilty? *Why* would I feel guilty? My husband was ruining our marriage, my life, the kids' lives with his drinking. But, like many a human emotion, guilt is neither logical nor rational. Allow the guilt without allowing it to interfere with your plans. Remember: you are not *leaving*. You are preparing to give yourself the choice to leave.

Just because you are working toward the day when you *can* leave, doesn't mean you *have* to leave. Living in an alcoholic marriage because you are choosing to stay feels a lot different than living in an alcoholic marriage because your choices are shackled to his life. Also, consider this:

You are in a better place to support him, be it financially, emotionally or physically, if you feel like a whole person living the best life she can. Your patience, your kindness, your stamina and your emotional generosity will be greater for the act of creating a life where you have the freedom to make your own choices.

Additionally, no matter what happens.

Whether you leave and he gets worse.

Or you stay and he gets worse.

Or you leave and he gets better.

Or you stay and he gets better.

Whatever happens in his life, is not your responsibility.

Even if you are his wife.

We all have our own paths to walk, our own choices to make, our own consequences to bear.

Absolve yourself of being responsible for his life. His choices. His path. Yes, a thousand times yes, it is sad and tragic and heartbreaking to walk away from someone who is destroying himself. It feels cruel to leave someone who's, it seems, only chance of a "healthy" or "normal" life is tied to you.

But the truth is you can't save him from his drinking.

You can only save yourself from it.

LESSON #9

Accept That Your Husband Is an Alcoholic — and Then Let It Go

Success if determined not by whether or not you face obstacles, but by your reation to them. And if you look at these obstacles as a containing fence then they become your excuse for failure. But if you look at them as a hurdle, each one stregthens you for the next.
Ben Carson, Gifted Hands: The Ben Carson Story

I spent a long time hating that my husband was an alcoholic.

A long, long time.

Too long.

It sucks being married to an alcoholic.

It really, really, *really* sucks.

You get drug down into the tar pit of his behavior and one day you realize: you are dangerously close to being more like him than not. You may not be drinking like him but the anger and rage and resentment you've long noticed in him is creeping into your being like a noxious, invasive vine.

I knew...

I felt...

I heard in my own words, the tone of my voice, my impatience and my outbursts, that I was becoming him.

And I blamed him and his drinking.

I knew it was because of him and his drinking.

I could feel it was because of him and his drinking.

But one day I started giving into the fact that my husband is an alcoholic.

I began accepting the marriage I had (which was most definitely not the one I wanted).

I began accepting the marriage I didn't have (the one I most definitely did want).

I started slowing sniping the strands that tethered me to him.

I thought they were made of steel.

It turns out they were only cotton.

I did not do this out of any grand plan or divine wisdom.

I was just tired.

So very, very, very tired.

Acceptance isn't approval.

Acceptance isn't complicity.

Acceptance isn't even resignation.

Not for your life anyway.

It is a resignation for the life and path your husband has chosen, whether it's forever or just-for-now.

I believed for so long the corrosion and destruction of my soul was due to his drinking.

And it was.

But it was also do to the battle I was waging daily within myself against his drinking.

You have to let it go.

Easy to say.

Hard to do.

And a lot of work.

I vividly remember the first time I made the conscious choice to "let go" of my own internal fight against my husband's compulsive drinking. I can still see where I was standing in my kitchen; I can still feel the rage I had to force down. The kitchen was a mess, as it always was. I was cleaning it up after having made dinner, as I always did. My husband walked in, took a beer out of the refrigerator and headed off to sit in front of the television.

I felt like a maid.

Angry bile began churning within me.

I could quite literally feel the rage physically within my body.

I closed my eyes, took a deep breath and mumbled out loud,

"He has his own path to lead. He has his own path to lead. His path is not my path. His path is not my path."

It was not pretty but it did turn out to be relatively effective.

I say "relatively" because it was more like choking down liver than eating creamy ice cream.

But it worked.

I was able to clean the kitchen without slamming pots into the cupboard or throwing utensils into the drawer. But I wasn't really "accepting."

But that's ok.

It's the place you have to start.

An awkward, liver-gagging, mind-over-rage, will-over-reality, choking it down, forcing your mind to try a new route. You have to actually train your brain to create new, healthier and more beneficial neuro-pathways. It's well understood and documented that addiction physically changes the addict's brain. It's why it makes recovery excruciatingly difficult. There are true, chemical reactions within the addict's brain not just calling him to drink/smoke/shoot up but basically demanding it. What isn't talked about is how your brain, as the wife of an addict, has physically changed too. It's created its own chemical reactions that call for, demand, certain reactions within you, just as in the alcoholic. When my husband brushed by me in the kitchen as I cleaned up from the dinner I had cooked, beer in his hand and focused on getting back to his beloved television, that rage I felt wasn't all "in my head." It was a real chemical reaction and it took a focused, conscious thought on my part to over-ride a chemically supported, habituated reaction.

In other words, the effort and process to change your reaction to your husband's drinking and behavior is going to feel maddening and forced and even painful at first but it is what is necessary in order to cultivate acceptance within yourself. For me, closing my eyes, taking deep breaths and repeating my mantra, "It's his path... this is not my path... it's his path," got me through my initial efforts.

Additionally, not allowing myself to continue to use his drinking as an excuse for what I didn't like in my life solidified my acceptance. I can't say this enough: it took a lot of work. And if I were to put some sort of quantitative number on "how long" it took me, I'd venture that it was probably a good five years. Not five years of being angry and resentful and bitter. Not five years of hating his drinking and wishing my marriage was different and cursing that it wasn't. Not five years of believing if my husband *just* wasn't an alcoholic, myself and my life would be so different. No, that was more like 20+ years. Practically from the very beginning of my marriage, when I first came to realize what was going on with him and alcohol, I became entangled in the web of his alcoholism.

I tried to free myself.

For a long time.

But I was like Sisyphus, forever pushing my own boulder of hate, anger, bitterness and resentment up a hill. You're never going to change anything in your life or within yourself through hating his drinking. Trust me. I tried. For too long. Misery is actually not a very sustainable or even powerful motivator. One of my favorite Aesop's Fables is about an argument between the sun and the wind. Each was arguing that they were the strongest. They saw a man walking along wearing a coat and decided that whoever could get the man to take off his coat was, indeed, the most powerful.

The wind went first.

It started to blow on the man, who then pulled his coat close to himself. As the wind blew harder, the man held onto his coat tighter. Harder and harder the wind blew; tighter and tighter the man held his coat until the wind was exhausted.

When it was the sun's turn to try, the sun simply began to rise in the sky, softly warming the man. The higher the sun rose, the warmer the man felt until he gently took his coat off.

Rallying against your husband's drinking is like the wind trying to blow a man's coat off.

It won't work and you'll just tire yourself out.

Acceptance is the sun.

Be the sun.

PART II
The Metaphysical

(aka Lessons from a Lost Cat)

LESSON #1

Believe in Something

The Universe is not outside of you.
Look inside yourself; everything that you want, you already are.
Rumi

I don't know what your beliefs are in the religious or spiritual sense and I say this with all sincere kindness:

I don't care.

Too many wars have been waged, lives lost and Thanksgiving dinners ruined by people caring what other people believe — and then trying to convince them they are wrong.

I grew up in what I would say was a mildly religious household. As children my mother took us to Sunday school and she attended church, though my father didn't. When we were of the age to be confirmed, we were confirmed but after that, it was our choice whether to stay with the church or not. My siblings left. I stayed until college and then slowly drifted away. As a mother now with children of the age that it's "too late" to introduce them to church, I kind a wished I had followed my mother's example but that will just have to be another one for the "regret box."

As the business of raising children and living with the realities of an alcoholic husband became my life, neither church nor any real kind of "belief" was part of that life. I attended a few different churches here and there over the years, but nothing really stuck for me. I liked to say I was "spiritual but not religious" though what did that even mean? I'm sure you've heard this claim before and while

I would never speak for anyone else, for me that statement meant absolutely nothing. I wasn't doing anything "spiritual." I wasn't engaging in or practicing anything that supported this "spirituality" of mine. I wasn't learning or exploring what it meant to me to be "spiritual." I was just trying to get from one day to the next, slowing dying in an alcoholic marriage.

Like everything else I have learned about how to survive, while trying to thrive, in an alcoholic marriage, stumbling into a focused spiritual practice came by accident and out of my despair. One day I decided to write "God" a letter. I don't know why. (Yes I do. Desperation.) I even began the letter "Not sure if I believe in you..." In this first letter, I asked for help. Begged for help. Of course, to many this would be called "prayer" and it doesn't matter to me how anyone labels it. The power was in reaching out beyond myself, into the vast unknown and unseen, in search of a power/force/energy greater than myself. Not of me but also, of me.

As I wrote my letters to God, sometimes quite blasphemous and damning of him/her/it (though he/she/it seemed to be able to shoulder it), something of a spiritual practice began to emerge for me. I began to meditate, read about Buddhist monks and explore what is considered the metaphysical. Finding your own way to a religious or spiritual practice and belief system is not unique to the wife of an alcoholic. But I will offer you this: as I reached outside my own physical and human existence and searched for what, I suppose some might call the "meaning of life," I found what I didn't even know had been missing through all those years of despair and desperation.

Little is more isolating than life with an addict. And often those that we turn to, our friends and family, are not necessarily a source of strength, renewal or growth. They may be supportive.

Staunchly, unwaveringly supportive but what I realized is my friends and family, in their desire to be what they thought was "supportive," actually inadvertently and out of no fault of their own, provided the high dive from which I dove deeper into my own misery and unhappiness. They allowed me bitch and complain all I wanted, under the guise of letting me "vent." The problem is eventually venting isn't cathartic or productive. Eventually venting is indulgent and defeatist and self-sabotaging.

Today I have what I call my "al a carte" spiritual practice. I believe in reincarnation. I believe we are spiritual beings living a physical life. I believe that the God anyone may seek — by any name or label — is far beyond anything that can be quantified while also, in the simplest terms, of each of us. I'm not telling you to "become religious" or "spiritual." I am certainly not suggesting that I have any grand answers as to what or who "God" or "Ala" or "Jesus" or "The Universe" may be. With every ounce my being, I believe every single person's theological beliefs are sacred of and not to be debated or dismissed by anyone else. I'm just offering, if the beliefs you once held dear have fallen away in the chaos of living in an alcoholic household or you have never really explored any religious, spiritual or philosophical approach or basis for life, finding yourself with an alcoholic husband might just be a reason to set out on your own sacred journey.

LESSON #2

Lessons from a Lost Cat

*When you want something, all the universe conspires
in helping you to achieve it.*
Paulo Coelho, The Alchemist

I suppose the field of metaphysics best describes my spiritual beliefs and practices. The word "metaphysics" is derived from the Greek word "meta," which means "beyond" and "physics," which means "of the physical." So, metaphysics is "beyond the physical." All the greats — Aristotle, Plato, Socrates dabbled in, if you will, the study of metaphysics. But for modern times and the majority of us, metaphysics came to the forefront of society's collective consciousness and rushing into our living rooms in 2006 with the publication of a little book called, "The Secret."

Based on the Law of Attraction, the book got, if not everyone — at least millions according to book sales — dialed into the idea that you can change your life by simply changing your thoughts. The Law of Attraction contents that if you *think about* receiving that new car, job offer or love interest, eventually you will. Of course, not the book, nor the Law of Attraction and certainly not the field of metaphysics is that simple but it was the easiest and quickest thing to take away from the book. Sadly, many abandoned both their dream of a new car/house/job/changed life and the field of metaphysics for a lot of people when simply "thinking about" those things didn't bring them to fruition.

It's sad that the real power in the Law of Attraction was lost.

As Dr. Wayne Dyer puts it, "you don't attract what you want. You attract what you are."

The (grossly simplified) idea behind both the Law of Attraction and metaphysics is our thoughts create and shape our realities; our realities don't create and shape our thoughts. However, no where I would dare to venture, is it easier to get lost to the latter than in an alcoholic marriage. Of course, you are miserable, stressed out, depressed, anxious, volatile and overwhelmed because your husband is an alcoholic. Your miserable, stressed out, depressed, anxious, volatile and overwhelmed thoughts didn't create your husband's alcoholism.

No, no they didn't.

Not in the least.

Your husband came to his compulsive drinking all on his own.

But is it possible you could create a reality for your life that was protected from his drinking? A reality that had its own "force field" around so that his chaos didn't invade the space of your life? Maybe.

When I was writing the first edition of this book, there came a period of several months where I just couldn't pull anything out of myself. No ideas would come, no words would flow even though I knew my ideas and I knew what I wanted to say. If that sounds oddly contradictory, it is. Such is the internal world of a writer. Of course, while I was stuck in the cement of my writer's block, my life marched on, requiring me to participate.

At the time, we had a neighbor, Mrs. Welsh who was about the loveliest creature you can imagine. She was then in her 70's, widowed and seemed to radiate nothing but kindness and gentleness no matter when you happened to see her.

She had a dear little cat — Lucky Lucy — who was the world to her. If you saw Mrs. Welsh out, you saw Lucky Lucy. The cat was everywhere Mrs. Welsh was. Sitting on her porch, "fussing" (as she liked to call it) in her garden, taking a walk around the block. Yes, the cat went for walks with its mistress! That cat, my family would say, "had the life."

One day "Lucy," as was her name initially, got out on her own and went missing.

Mrs. Welsh was desperate with fear to find her and the whole neighborhood searched daily for her. After four very long days, Lucy decided to return on her own and there she was one morning, sitting on the porch as though nothing had ever happened. Lucy became forever known as "Lucky Lucy," having safely returned amidst all the dangers — both real and imagined by her human friends.

One day, Mrs. Welsh came to my daughter and explained that her family was taking her on a cruise to celebrate her upcoming birthday. She wanted to know if my daughter would cat-sit Lucky Lucy. My daughter was more than willing to do so but everything in me was screaming,

"NO!"

I don't know why my internal self was so against it.

Actually, yes I do know why.

I had seen and felt the heartache and despair — and while especially in Mrs. Welch but not just Mrs. Welsh. My whole family, the entire neighborhood — we were all frantic with worry about that little cat. For those excruciating 96 hours, no one greeted each other without initially asking,

"Has Lucy been found?"

My kids would arrive home from school,

"Did you find Lucy?" (No pressure there.)

What if something "happened while my daughter was cat-sitting? What if Lucky Lucy snuck out again on my daughter's watch? I certainly wanted my daughter to be a kind neighbor, but I feared that degree of responsibility for her. It's hard to argue irrational mom-fear with a daughter though and I didn't want to confide my concerns to Mrs. Welsh, so my only choices seemed to be say "yes" or risk coming off as a mean, neurotic neighbor and mother.

The first five or six days were fine. Uneventful. Lucky Lucy was accounted for every morning at breakfast time and every night for dinner and bed time. I did gently express some concern to Mrs. Welch

— blaming it on mom-neurosis (rightfully so?) — about Miss. Lucky Lucy giving my daughter the slip and so a plan was created:

We put a litter box in Mrs. Welch bedroom so my daughter could lock Lucky Lucy in the bedroom before she even so much as touched the door knob to leave the house. YouTube videos not withstanding, most cats can't or don't open doors so I felt confident with this approach. Additionally, (though I didn't share this with Mrs. Welch) I refused to let my daughter go tend the cat alone. She was annoyed by this, as you can imagine. I mean, really, really, *really* annoyed and secretly I didn't know that I could blame her.

One night, about a week or so into this ten day cat-sitting gig, I was in the middle of doing something when my daughter wanted to go take care of Lucky Lucy.

I told her she needed to wait til I was done with what I was doing.

"I can do it, mom," she said, with more than a little annoyance in her voice.

Even I had to admit I was being a little over-zealous with my feline-diligence and acquiesced though not without first a litany of warnings.

Don't go out in Mrs. Welsh's backyard.

Don't open any doors other then when you walk in.

Don't forget to put her in the bedroom when you leave.

Etc., etc., etc.

"I know!" My daughter responded impatiently and off she went.

The next morning my daughter was sleeping in and I told her I would go check on the cat.

With my coffee cup in hand, I happily strolled across the street to Mrs. Welsh's house, looking forward to some time away from the chaos of my own home and life,

I walked into the house, went confidently to Mrs. Welsh's bedroom, calling out my presence to Lucky Lucy as I opened the bedroom door though the question of "did I open it or was it open?" would come to plague me.

"Hi kitty kitty," I said cheerily.

My eyes scanned the room, expecting to see her laying on the bed or chair.

"Kitty?" I called, curious but not overly concerned.

"Lucky Lucy?" I said, more of a question than a call.

"Kitty?" I demanded, looking under the bed.

My heart began to race. I could feel my mind panicking. I started darting around the room, throwing the closet doors open, looking behind the bed, under the bed again and again. In the window sill, behind the dresser, under the chair, behind the curtains.

THE CAT WASN'T THERE!!

NO! NO! NO! NO! NO!

This was NOT happening!

I willed it not to be!

"FUCK. FUCK. FUCK. FUCK." I screamed to no one.

"OH MY GOD!" I yelled.

"OH MY FUCKING GOD!"

I ran out of the bedroom, through the house. She must have slipped out right as I opened the door and walked in.

"LUCY! LUCY! LUCY! LUCY!!!" I screamed through the house.

"Please dear God. PLEASE!"

As I write this now, it's hard to believe such panic arouse in me and yet I can feel that panic all over again, with the same intensity. As if I was right back there now.

I called my daughter.

"GET OVER HERE! LUCKY LUCY IS GONE!"

"What?" she asked in her sleepy state.

"DON"T WHAT ME! THE CAT IS GONE! YOU DIDN'T LISTEN! YOU NEVER LISTEN! YOU ALWAYS THINK YOU KNOW BETTER!"

It was horrible.

I was horrible.

Just awful.

I would prefer not to think about it, write about it or share it but it's the truth and the reality of where I was in my life then. My daughter walked into the house and what had started on the phone only intensified and worsen in person. I screamed at her,

"THE CAT IS FUCKIN GONE!"

I had NEVER talked to any of my children like that before.

"YOU DIDN'T CLOSE THE GOD DAMN DOOR!" I screamed.

"I did, Mom!" She kept saying. "I did! I did! I promise I did mom!"

And I kept screaming.

"YOU DIDN'T!! STOP SAYING YOU DID BECAUSE YOU DIDN'T!!! IF YOU HAD THE CAT WOULD BE HERE NOW AND IT'S NOT!! I'M SO MAD AT YOU!!!"

It was ugly, it was cruel, it was viscous. I am crying now as I write this and relive how I treated my child. I was completely out of control. Of course, it had nothing to do with the cat. Not really. Life in the alcoholic marriage is a 24 hour/seven day a week pressure cooker. I am not justifying or blaming my behavior on my alcoholic husband. The opposite really: we need to be aware of the intense stress we are under on a daily basis so that this sort of thing doesn't happen to us. So we aren't hijacked by that stress in an unrelated moment.

We looked everywhere for that cat, both in and out of the house. We looked in places a cat couldn't possible be and then looked in there again. My mind kept saying,

"It's ok. The cat is around here some place."

I've searched for — and found — a few lost cats in my day. I knew — intellectually anyway, when my mind isn't in full blown freak-out mode — that the most likely place for a cat who got outside by accident is within a couple hundred feet of exactly where you are looking for it. Indoor cats tend to hunker down and *hide* when they get out, not wander off. I knew that. But I allowed panic to repeatedly over take logically, rational thinking. I tried to calm myself down. I told myself all these things I knew as truths but just when it seemed my brain had hopped off that hot burner of panic, my head went to every bad place it could!

Car.

Coyote.

Thief.

After about two hours of searching, my daughter sheepishly reminded me she was suppose to go to a friend's house. By now I had composed myself and though still sick with panic, I was no longer mad at her.

I was mad at myself.

How could I have ever, ever, EVER spoken to my child that way?

Why did I go against my gut instinct and say "yes" in the first place?

I should have never become complacent and let my daughter go alone.

The irony is had it been my own cat while I may have been concerned, I would not have been so panic-stricken. But my mind kept bombarding me with thoughts of having to tell a little old widowed lady that we had lost her precious cat!

My daughter looked at me nervously.

I wanted her to go to her friend's house, I assured her. I told her I would stay and look for the cat. Guilt over my treatment of my daughter mixed with anxiety over the missing cat. There was no where for me to get away from my own emotions. I felt almost a physical pain. I continually returned to the bedroom, telling myself this was all just some kind of ridiculous oversight on our part and the cat was in there.

I finally accepted that I had looked all I could for the time being and went home.

For the rest of the day, I went back and forth to the house, hoping and praying the cat would magically reappeared. But the day dragged on. Three, four, five... SIX hours and still no cat!

I honestly feared I was going to give myself a stroke or heart attack, my anxiety was so consuming. Finally, around 7:00 o'clock that evening, I said to myself,

"I have got to do something."

What compelled me to do what I did, I have no idea but I opened up my laptop and googled, "how to ask the Universe to return lost pets."

(Yes, that's how desperate I was.)

But guess what?

The site and advice that seemed most promising was from the website, "realityshifters.com. I wrote down the six steps offered for how to "ask the Universe to return lost things" and went back to my neighbors house. I looked around one more time, in hope the cat had finally returned on its own and I wouldn't have to go through this arduous? Pointless? Task of asking the entire *Universe* to find a lost cat.

Calm down was the first step. Not surprising if you think about it. According to the site, being panicked, stressed and/or overly agitated creates an energy within you that disrupts the energy of the Universe, making it difficult, if not impossible for the Universe to help. Think of it like you are drowning and as someone tries to pull you to safety, you keep flailing about and hitting them in the head.

The next step was hope for a reality shift.

Then meditate.

Followed by feel your love for what you lost.

Let go.

And finally, appreciate the surprise reunion.

I focused my energy on all these steps.

Calm... meditate... reality shift... let go... love... reunion.

Calm... meditate... reality shift... let go... love... reunion.

Over and over again. Like trying to put together IKEA furniture with that one tiny Allen wrench they give you. (I was about that awkward too.)

And then...

After about 20 minutes of calming and meditating, letting go and loving the best I could, I thought I heard the faintest mew!

I am not making this up!

I froze, as if any movement on my part would somehow make it not so.

Did I really hear what I thought I heard?

"Kitty?" I said with guarded hope.

"Mew."

There it was again!

"Kitty?

"Mew."

"Kitty?"

"Mew."

Back and forth we went — kitty/mew, kitty/mew — as I was actually afraid to believe it was true. (Meanwhile the cat was probably thinking, "Ok, come on already!")

One more "kitty" check before I dared allowed myself to trust this was indeed happening.

"Kitty?"

"Mew."

Yep, the "mew" was definitely real and it was coming from the vicinity of an upholstered chair. A chair I had looked around and behind several times. A chair I had pushed away from the wall to check for her. A chair with barely any clearance between the bottom of it and the floor.

A chair that there was no way a cat could get under.

Or so I thought.

Despite the chair literally being just inches of the ground, Lucky Lucy had indeed flattened herself and crawled under it.

But that's not the only thing that had hampered our recovery efforts.

In our previous search efforts, apparently when I pushed the chair forward, the cat had either been pushed forward with it or chose to crawl forward with it. Or was the cat not even there initially? Did the Universe "put" her there? Sounds hokey and crazy I know but that doubt will always linger in my mind. Either way, this time, armed with the expectation of *finding her,* I tilted the chair up and gently ushered Lucky Lucy out with my foot.

Stupid cat.

I scooped her up, hugging her while also admonishing her for being such a bad kitty. Relief flooded my central nervous system where panic had once been.

And then I remembered my daughter.

Or more specifically, I remembered how ugly and cruel I had been to her.

To this day, I feel an unwavering shame over how I reacted and subsequently treated her. I knew it wasn't "just" the cat but that didn't make me feel better: it made me feel worse. What was happening to me? Who was I becoming? I could apologize — and of course I would — but what message did that send her? People who are meant to love you can be wickedly viscous as long as they say "I'm sorry" after wards?

Apologies are great for when you bump into someone or accidentally take their coffee at Starbucks or forget to return a phone call but after a verbally abusive tirade? Unleashed on a daughter by her mother?

I knew I would apologize but I also knew an apology was not enough.

I had to change.

I had been thinking I would change, saying I was going to change, even planning to change but I hadn't.

I'll never, ever *not* regret the way I treated my daughter but I am grateful for the lost cat.

As crazy and out-there, and perhaps even somewhat self-indulgent as it sounds, that incident showed me how to proceed with this book.

It told me what I had longed suspected but had yet committed to living by:

Call it God...

The Universe...

Allah...

Jehovah...

Life force or Energy, it doesn't matter.

What matters to me is that I reach for something in my life that is beyond my physical existence and survival. I would never even hint at telling anyone what they should believe or seek but I will offer you this from my own extended stay in the alcoholic marriage: You can become very insulated when married to an alcoholic. You're grieving your own marital losses. You're trying to contain or manage your own anger. If you have children, you're trying to protect them while also nurture them, which by the way is not easy. "Protect" and "nurture" tend to be somewhat mutually exclusive. Think of trying to survive the beach in the middle of a hurricane... while also trying to enjoy the ocean waves. And then there is the daily interactions with the alcoholic himself. You become all balled up inside. A big knot of conflicting emotions. You try, you really try but you keep going to the well-of-you that is depleted daily but refilled rarely. Friends and family aren't really much help. They tend to fall into two camps: indulging your need to complain or telling you to get the hell out. Neither is helpful for your own growth and healing.

Seek something beyond yourself. You are not meant to spend your days just clinging to this big, blue orb while it whirls around the sun. There is meant to be purpose and meaning to your life.

And if you go in search of that purpose with calm and a loving attitude.

And work to quiet the chatter through meditation...

While feeling love for a purpose as yet unrealized...

And live in the joy of finding (reuniting with) that purpose before you actually find it...

One day you just might hear the faintest of mews leading you to what may have been there all along.

LESSON #3

Choose a Different Way of Being in the Universe

You are the Universe, expressing yourself as a human for a little while.
Eckhart Tolle

As the saying goes, "when the student is ready, the teacher appears."

In my case, the teacher was a cat.

I would have appreciated the Universe perhaps using a different avenue. Say, one that didn't involve my apparent need to yell and curse at my child. But then, I myself have often said that when you don't first listen to the Universe, it is often forced to revert to more drastic measures to get your attention. The Universe had probably been tapping on my shoulder, trying to get me to take note of some guidance it wanted to impart upon me. But when I seemed to be refusing to respond, it went for something a little more dramatic. That couldn't be ignored. Of course, in the moment I wasn't like,

"Hmm? Maybe the Universe is trying to tell me something."

No, in that moment the lost cat and my alcoholic marriage seemed completely irrelevant to one another. Of course, you can't be flailing about — literally or metaphysically — and expect the Universe to be able to step in and work some of its metaphysical magic. Like a child who has fallen off her bike and is crying hysterically: mom can't tell if she needs a band aid or a trip to the ER. I could accept such doctrine as it applied to lost keys, missing wallets or wayward kitty cats.

But not when it came to alcoholic husbands.

Not when it came to my alcoholic husband and my life with him.

For nearly 20 years, I had believed that I needed to live from a place of chaos and turmoil.

Whenever my husband would fly into one of his "fuck you's" and "shut the fuck ups" rages, I would tell myself "hold onto this."

When he was in the darkest of his drinking moods, yelling and cursing over anything and everything, I'd think, "remember this!"

When his very presence would send a physical anxiety pulsating through my body, I'd try to will myself to keep that anxiety alive and active within myself.

When my head would scream, "I CAN'T LIVE LIKE THIS!" and I felt a visceral need to get out of my marriage, I'd encourage myself to "never forget" this depth of despair.

It seemed to make sense to me. Remembering how miserable I was in the worst of moments would motivate me to work harder in the better moments to get out, right?

Well, it just so happens that to try to live in a sustained sense of chaos and discord is about *the* worst thing you can do when you are trying to regain control of your life. When crisis strikes — be it an immediate threat like a lost cat or the more chronic condition of an alcoholic marriage — and bedlam is raging in the world outside of you, you can't be equally agitated and panicked, You can't be more of or contributing to the very disorder and discord you are trying to escape.

You have to be a calming force.

You have to be more focused.

You have to be emotionally and mentally un-agitated.

Your soul has to be still. Not dormant but still, centered. Quiet. You can't be rushing about — physically, mentally, emotionally or spiritually — like a goose on fire.

This just sets the rest of your life on fire.

It was after I found the cat that I began to notice how reactive I was to my husband and his behavior. If he left his trash laying around (as he always did), I would feel the resentment start to bubble up in me. When I'd come home from an entire day and evening of ferrying kids here and there and everywhere only to find him parked in front of the tv with the kitchen sink piled high with dirty dishes, anger would instantly overtake me. And when he would scream his ugly, viscous words at me, yes, I thought I should will myself to carry those heinous words in me forever. But the missing-cat-lesson turned life-lesson showed me how wrong, damaging, dangerous and even tragic such an attitude or approach is.

For the first time in probably ever I became aware of my reactions and I began to *choose* my reactions. When faced with the stress of my house, my family, my alcoholic husband and/or just life in general with an alcoholic present, I would repeat to myself,

"I choose to be in the Universe differently. I choose to be in the Universe differently."

I remember sometimes having to close my eyes and repeat my mantra over and over again before a sense of calm overtook the pull of the anxiety. Eventually though, it always (ALWAYS!) worked. Of course, I still had the kitchen to clean or his trash to put in the waste bin. And my mantra never once sobered him up. But it was the beginning of taking back control of my emotions, my reactions and my life.

It's clear our alcoholic husbands have made their choices on how they want to be in the Universe. And as the wives of alcoholics, most of us inadvertently choose how we are going to be in the Universe by default, in our responses to their choices. But those aren't choices. They are knee-jerk reactions. Reactions born out of habit and shortsightedness. Reactions born out of a sense of justification. Yes, there is no question any woman married to an alcoholic is justified in her reactions of anger and resentment, sadness and grief.

The problem is "justified" does not allow you to seek and create your best life.

"Justified" does not promote good mental, emotional or physical health.

"Justified" does not take you down the beautiful path of your own unique journey.

"Justified" is a big, giant sign at the edge of an ominous jungle trail warning "DANGER! DO NOT ENTER!"

"Justified" creates dangerous, destructive reactions with devastatingly long-term consequences .

And not just for you.

For the Universe.

For your place in the Universe.

Because what you put out in the Universe is what the Universe sends back to you. It's not that the Universe is vindictive or retaliatory. But for all its beautiful magic and divine power, it can only work with what you give it. You wouldn't give your Nana mud and rocks and expect her to create her county fair-blue-ribbon-winning-50-years-in-a-row-and-counting apple pie.

It's impossible to align with the Universe and create and allow good things in your life when you are in a continued state of anxiety, distress, agitation and resentment. And when in an alcoholic marriage for any length of time, this state can be so persistent and continual as to start to feel "normal." Your default way of being in your life, within yourself.

And in the Universe.

Except not really.

The tragically dangerous thing that is happening within you is though you may cease to be fully aware of this stress on a daily basis, in the conscious sense, that stress does not cease to exist. Nor does it cease to exert its ill effects upon you. Your body *feels* this stress. Your body is *reacting* biochemically to this stress. And guess what this biochemical reaction influences?

The energy you put out into the Universe.

And guess what responds to this energy?

Yes.

The Universe.

We are not inanimate objects with no effect on the world around us. Life is not a passive ride. On the day you were born, cosmic forces didn't strap you into an Earth-bound buggy with the directive,

"HOLD ON!"

No, this ride we call Life is highly interactive.

You are energy and that energy (aka you) goes beyond the confines of your physical body and personal space and into the Universe. Energy is a boomerang so whatever you throw out there, is going to come right back to you. You wouldn't throw a blue boomerang and expect a red one to come sailing back around.

That's the bad news in regards to negative energy, stressed energy, anxious energy.

The good news is that when we change our energy, when we change how we are being in the Universe, when we work to live and exist in the positive and the affirmative, that too goes past us and far into the Universe at large. With beautiful, life changing results! It's not easy at first. It's awkward and can feel a little "fake" or "false." I had to make a conscious effort to change my thoughts and my reactions. But that's ok. That's how change works in the beginning. Big, jerky, awkward movements. It gets easier. Automatic. Becomes part of your being.

One of my favorite sayings is, "you can't steal second with your foot on first."

And you can't exist in the negative while expecting the positive to arrive. I know (I know, I know, I know... I! KNOW!) the searing pain and the debilitating *suck* of being married to an alcoholic. And I lived in that pain and suck for a long, long, long... LONG time. In fact, I felt quite justified living in the pain and suck. And I probably was, just as you are. No one can doubt or blame you for hating marriage to an alcoholic.

But...

There is no way to take back your life, gain control of your destiny, live to your fullest potential *and* stay in that darkness. After all, no one ever made it across home by staying on first.

LESSON #4

Ask the Universe for a Money-Reality Shift

Since money is energy, our financial affairs tend to reflect how our life energy is moving. When your creative energy is flowing freely, often your finances are as well. If your energy is blocked, your money does too.
Shakti Gawain

For a lot of us, one of the things that keeps us in our marriages is finances.

Or should I say, lack of finances as in lack of financial freedom from our husbands. This is not necessarily true for all wives of alcoholics — and just because a woman may have the financial means to leave her husband doesn't mean coming to the decision to leave him is an emotional slam dunk for her. But if and when you add money challenges — as was the case for me — it becomes nearly impossible to move forward with your life. That nasty little dollar-sign of doom has a way of sitting on your shoulder and paralyzing you with its taunts.

"Yeah, but you have no money."

"How are you going to leave him with no money?"

"What are you going to do for money?"

"Money money money money money money money money money money," it ranted in my ear, over and over and OVER again.

For years.

It became a vicious cycle.

I'd feel powerful and hopeful, capable and ready to begin

separating my life from his. I'd start making the choices and taking the physical actions necessary to create the life I wanted. But then...

The money-beast would start its yacking and derail me. I'd give up, quit, feel defeated before I really tried until something in me was ignited once again. My drive, my confidence, my will would come rushing back to me and I'd be off again. Oh yes, I was going to do it this time! I was going to create my own financial freedom, build the life I longed for...

Then there it was again.

That voice.

Yack, yack, yack, yack, yack about how was I going to do this when I had no money, no "real" job... blah blah blah blah blah.

And I'd be down again.

But then the (now proverbial) lost cat...

And the fortuitous googling of "how to get the Universe to return lost things...

And the random (random?) website "RealityShifts.com.

And suddenly my financial concerns were solved.

Really.

Before even a dime more found its way into my bank account.

Now, I warn you this is one of those that is going to sound *way out there*. As you're reading it, you may be tempted to think,

"Yeah, right I would LOVE to just ask the Universe for more money but it doesn't seem to work that way."

No, no it doesn't.

You can't ask the Universe for money — or even a money reality shift — and have someone knock at your door the next day with a bag of cash, cart full of silver or a treasure chest of gold bullion.

But...

You can ask the Universe for a money-reality shift, physically work toward that end and *then* have money seem to "suddenly" appear in your life.

It worked for me.

Really.

First, the manager at the store where I was working part-time quit. That meant the assistant manager became manager and I was asked to be a "shift supervisor," which meant more money and more hours. Now, I know what you may be thinking.

"So the Universe "gave" you more money by making you work more hours? That hardly seems so miraculous or metaphysical."

Hey, like I said, we all have to do the *physical work* in order for the Universe to funnel money into our lives. Besides, the "more hours at the store" did more than just give me more cash. It created a variety of "coincidences" or "happenstance" meetings and encounters which in turn created all sorts of opportunities for my writing, art and other creative endeavors.

The Universe, God, Allah — whatever title or label you care to give the energy force that lies both beyond us but also within us — wants you to have the things you want. Money, for all the baggage us humans have heaped on it, is not that big a deal to the Universe. "You want money?" The Universe asks. "Fine. I can arrange for you to have money."

The problem is we tend to block or limit the ways in which the Universe can channel money to us. We may believe in prayer when it comes to healing or getting a job or our favorite team winning the Super Bowl but prayer... asking for *money*? That's downright blasphemous.

From the website, "RealityShifters" in regards to asking the Universe to return lost things, Cynthia writes that you should hope for a "reality shift." A reality shift is just as it says; a shift in what you know to be "reality." As Cynthia says, in that way, the Universe is free to return your lost item to you in whatever way is most convenient — for the Universe. Maybe in a place you've already searched "100 times." Or maybe in a location that makes you scratch your head and wonder "how the hell did it end up there?" Regardless, when you stop requiring the Universe return your lost object in a way that makes sense to you and allow the Universe to return it in a way that makes

sense to It, you've freed an infinite number of routes for your keys/
phone/camera/favorite earrings/wayward cat to come back to you.

And so it is when you ask for a shift in your money-reality.

As participants in this thing called life on this sphere called Earth,
we have all agreed to certain laws of physics. Like dollar bills don't
suddenly materialize out of thin air. Maybe on another sphere in
another life with a different set of physical laws, that does happen
but here, we have our laws to abide by. And in choosing this sphere
to hang out on, you and me, we agreed to these laws long before we
were even conscious of such. But that doesn't mean the Universe
can't, doesn't or won't find creative ways to channel money to you
while keeping it real with our physics here on Earth.

The Universe is your rich uncle, your wealthy grandma and Santa
Clause all rolled up in one.

Remember, to the Universe, money isn't money.

Money is energy and the Universe has plenty of money-energy
and it wants you to have it.

Of course, it's not going to just "hand" you money, with the whole
world watching. Just like the humans, the Universe needs to stay true
to and honor the Earthly physical laws we all accepted as a condition
of this ultimate amusement park called Life on Earth. It'd be like
when you were a kid, your rich, eccentric, uncle trying to hand you
$500 bucks with your mom and dad watching.

"Oh no! You're not going to just give her money like that, Uncle
Deep Pockets. She needs to learn the value of a dollar, the pride of
working hard..."

Blah, blah, blah, blah, blah.

Just like that, your childhood dreams of a pony are dashed.

But Uncle (generous) Deep Pockets isn't easily detered.

So he pays you $500 to walk his dog.

"You said," he says with a wink and a sly smile as he throws your
mom and dad's words back at them, "she needed to learn to work for
money."

Just like your rich Uncle Deep Pockets, the Universe works around Earth's physical laws to channel money to you through the metaphysical.

It creates chance encounters ("chance..." encounters), coincidences ("coincidences") and all sorts of serendipitous happenings (some you may never even bear witness to!) that bring you and money together.

You happen ("happen") to meet someone who is hiring for the exact same position you have been searching for. You run into someone who is looking for what your company sells. You meet someone who is in the field you've been wanting to switch over to. It's hard to come up with examples because the Universe has ways and means that you and I cannot even *imagine*. Crazy ways. Out of this world means that would sound hooky and unbelievable if you read them on paper.

Money is a weird thing for a lot of us but it's nothing weird for the Universe. It's just another form of energy and the Universe's attitude is,

"OK. If that's how you humans want to run the amusement park of Life, I'll play along."

I definitely have had serious struggles with letting money into my life. It seemed so... *greedy*. And yet, I never begrudged others their good financial fortune. And I didn't begrudge myself good health, friendship or love. But money?

Yep, somehow I seemed undeserving. I remember when I first started thinking about making a living at writing, this nasty little gremlin shouted in my head,

"Yeah?! Who are you to get to support yourself with writing?! Lots of people would like to live that life."

OUCH!

I firmly believe for me, these conflicting feelings about good old cash contributed to my many years of feeling stagnant and stuck in my marriage. I needed out. I wanted out. At times, I thought, *I am going to die if I don't get out*, and yet I repeatedly interrupted my own journey to financial freedom. If your feelings about money resemble mine or if you have your own convoluted, limiting beliefs about yourself and money, my best advice to you is change that now. Stop thinking of money as a limited well that only a few are invited to drink from. Money is simply one more form of energy and as a card-carrying human with an all-inclusive ticket to Earth, you are entitled to, deserve and can have all the financial abundance you desire.

No, money is not going to magically appear in your bank account. But once I asked for and opened myself up to a money-reality shift, good things began happening for me. Some involved a blatant increase in my earnings but others were a more windy road but a road none the less. A road to financial abundance and freedom that hadn't been there before.

Depending on your own beliefs and/or how you grew up, you too may be stuck with allowing financial abundance into your life. I struggled my entire adult life with feeling it was ok to want money, a lot of money frankly. I had to stop seeing money as some mystical demi-God, unavailable to most of us and start seeing (knowing) it for the energy form it is. You deserve money-energy in your life every bit as much as you deserve the other forms of energy life has to offer — love, harmony, stamina, passion, physical health. It's ok to invite it and allow it in.

LESSON #5

Learn from the Rice and Water

Whatever you resist you become
If you resist anger, you are always angry.
If you resist sadness, you are always sad.
If you resist suffering, you are always suffering.
If you resist confusion, you are always confused.
We think we resist certain states because they are there, but actually
they are there because we resist them.
Adyashanti

I hope you visit "realityshifters.com." My next story didn't come from Cynthia's cite but you'll find a lot of valuable and interesting information on her website, blog and in the books she's written regarding living life beyond the physical boundaries we falsely believe govern and confine us. Remember, preparing to leave your alcoholic husband isn't about leaving your alcoholic husband at all: it's about becoming an active creator of you own destiny — rather than a passive participant on the runaway train you interadvetanly boarded when you married an alcoholic.

Have you ever considered how negative your daily thoughts are?

How, no matter if it's your husband or your appearance or your kids or your house or your dog or your life in general, it's nearly automatic, and virtually 100% of the time, that your internal response is negative?

What do you say to yourself when you catch a passing glimpse of yourself in the mirror?

What thought pops into your head when you walk into the kitchen, bathroom, living room, family room, bed rooms or any other room in your house and see the piles of laundry, dirty dishes, random clutter?

What thoughts bombard your mind when you see the beer bottles stacking up or watch your husband pour himself one more "one more?"

For me, sadly, it was always thoughts like,

"GOD! I am so fat!"

"I look SO old."

"I'm so tired looking!"

Or,

"NO ONE DOES SHIT AROUND HERE!"

"I hate this house!"

"I can't live like this one minute longer!"

These, and others not any kinder, were the words that ricoheted around in my head on a daily basis. A nearly-continous stream of dream-annihilating, soul-crushing, passion-withering mental chatter whispering (shouting, nagging, crying) in my ear from virtually sun up to sun down. And often beyond as going to bed at night did not necessarily bring about a quiet reprieve.

There is a man in Japan, Dr. Masaru Emoto, who teaches and works in the metaphysical field. He conducted an experiment with water where he directed negative, disparaging thoughts at one sample of water and positive, affirmative thoughts toward another. He then froze the water and with some crazy-advanced, complicated photography-techniques, photographed the crystals that had formed.

The "positive" water had formed beautiful, symmetrical and snowflake-like crystals where as the "negative" water had formed "ugly," asymmetrical and blotchy crystals.

Dr. Emoto did a similar experiment with rice where he set out two containers of cooked rice. On one container he wrote "I love you." On the other, he wrote "I hate you." Then for 30 days he had school children say warm, kind words to the "I love you" rice and mean, nasty words to the "I hate you" rice. At the end of 30 days the "I love you" rice was still white, plump and healthy looking where as the "I hate you" rice was growing black mold and fungus and could be said to look disease ridden.

Dr. Emoto works extensively to show that our thoughts and feelings do impact the physical world we inhabit. His work is not without its doubters or critics. Obviously I am not one of them. But even if you want to doubt, question or find fault with his work (and the abundance of evidence and work by others that supports the "crazy" idea that the metaphysical realm is very much real and active in the human experience), ask yourself this:

"Does the constant barrage of negative chatter in my head serve me or my life?"

"Is my life *better* for all the crap I listen to from my own psyche every day?"

"Do all the negative, pessimistic thoughts I think every day lift me up?"

I'm pretty sure the answers are, in no particular order, "no," "no" and "no."

There is an abundance of awareness these days as to the affect our mental and emotional states have on the physical state of our lives. We can no longer pretend that the two are separate, with one having no bearing on the other. Your life is profoundly (PROFOUNDLY!) affected by your thoughts and as the wife of an alcoholic, your thoughts are profoundly (PROFOUNDLY!) affected by your husband. It seems that as human beings, it is practically our "default" mode to take in the behavior of those around us and transform it into our own internal story.

To change this takes a conscious, deliberate effort and continued practice.

It takes countering the negative with the positive — even if you don't necessarily "believe" the positive at first.

For years (YEARS!) I would see my reflection in the mirror and think something like,

"I'm so fat."

"I look so old."

"God, I look tired."

"What happened to me."

Nice, huh?

I had to make a deliberate effort to counter these thoughts. I started "responding" with thoughts like,

"You are beautiful!"

"You look so joyful and at peace!"

"Your body is in amazing shape!"

Sometimes I'd even say these things out loud to myself!

Yep, it feels awkard, even fake sometimes.

But you should still do it.

(Why is it we have no problem saying horrific, debilitating, mean things to ourselves but when someone suggests we say nice, loving things, it seems "silly," "awkward" and "fake?"

An alcoholic husband will affect you in Every. Single. Way. possible. Mentally, phyically, emotionally and spiritually. He will erode your sense of being and decay your wonder and passion for living. If your desire and goal is to create a life of your choosing, a life of financial independence and options based on your desire — not your circumstances — then you really must start being aware of the things you say to yourself and then work to correct them. (Unless you've already figured this out and spend your days complimenting yourself and basking in the glow of your own self-recognized and celebrated grandness. In that case, just keep doing what you're doing.)

If you're still not convinced.

If you think "that is fine for other women but I am really am fat... broke... defeated... a loser, consider this:

Would you ever (ever!) say to a friend or a loved one as they headed off to an important job interview,

"You'll do great! I know you can do this! They'll be lucky to hire you..."

"Though you know, you look really fat in that outfit. And when did the wrinkles around your eyes become so noticeable?"

Would you tell your child, as he packed his bags for college,

"I'm so very proud of you."

"You'll probably fail out. You know you're not that smart and you didn't really work as hard as you could have in high school but have a great freshman year."

Of course, this sounds absurd!

Who on Earth would *ever* say such things to someone they loved and wanted to support and encourage? And yet, these are the sorts of things — and worse — that many of us say to ourselves on a daily basis.

It's very sad, isn't it? When you start listening, as an outside observer, to yourself talking to yourself.

You and I both know how much it sucks, suck, sucks, SUCKS to live with an alcoholic husband in an alcoholic household. In our world, a "good" night can be him passed out in front of the televsion. A bad night? Well, there is sadly no end to the possibilities for a bad night.

We know the maddening frustration of being with a partner who is not a partner. A parnter who feels like an open tap from which the very marrow of our soul is draining out rather than a partner who renews us, refills the well of our being.

We know (we KNOW!) how much we hate his compulsive drinking and accompanying behavior. With every proton of every atom of every cell of ever fiber of our being, we hate being married to an alcoholic.

And we know how much it hurts to watch not only his decline into the abyss of alcohlism but our own fall into an abyss not even of our choosing.

It's time to arrest that fall.

Like a grabling hook thrust into the side of a cliff, changing your thoughts can nearly-instantly stop your free fall.

Make a conscious effort (every! Day!) to counter your negative thoughts. You will probably feel silly or awkward, maybe even a little like a fraud but, like any endeavor, you'll get better with practice.

Now, if I catch a glimpse of mysel in the mirror, I refuse to hear those cruel, horrible words I once spoke to myself. Instead, I say things like,

"Wow! You look so joyful! You're body is so healthy and fit!"

If I see a house that is cute and adorable, I replace the old "wow, I wish I could have a house like that" with "I can buy that house if I want..."

You may think this is all metaphysical, woo-hoo, gobbly-gook but ask yourself a couple questions:

First, is your current mod-a-operand working for you? Are all the ugly, negative, defeatist thoughts helping you create the life of your dreams? Do these thoughts, ideas and beliefs motivate you?

Or shackle you?

Your alcoholic husband and marriage may have put the shackles on you but your own thoughts are the key to unlocking them.

The second question to ask yourself is this:

It may be metaphysical, woo-hoo, gobbly-gook but what if it's not? What if it's real and true and life really does operate like this?

I truly believe life exists and operates on a metaphysical plane that we are just now coming to be aware of and understand. For me, there is no doubt that we are all of infinite power and that this power aligns with something even more powerful — the Universe.

I also believe that harnessing or tapping into that power begins with our own thoughts. It's what finally worked for me! Once I divorced myself from my old beliefs and halted the emotional and mental knee jerk reaction I had to pretty much everything in my life, things began to change for me. There was a shift in my internal state of being as well as the physicality of my existence.

Frankly, I felt a little foolish to have ever believed it could have ever been the other way around. That my husband and my house and my finances had to change *first* before my emotions and mental state could. It took me 20 years to get this. I hope it doesn't take you quite as long.

LESSON #6

Align Yourself with a Higher Power
(And Give It Permission to Come into Your Life)

Look at the sky. We are not alone. The whole universe is friendly to us and conspires only to give the best to those who dream and work.
A.P.J. Abdul Kalam

Ok, I know this metaphysical stuff can sound *out there* but think of it this way: nothing about the "default" mode of living life with an alcoholic husband does much to help you take control of your life and create the life of your dreams. Without a conserted effort to the contrary, the alcoholic marriage leaves us approaching life through the lens of anger and resentment, bitterness and grief. So why not try the "crazy" stuff? Because truth be told, what is crazier:

Asking the Universe for help?

Or spending your life being called a "fucking bitch," searching for hidden booze bottles and praying tonight is a peaceful one?

Beside this is *so easy*.

Ask.

Believe.

Act.

Repeat.

Every morning before I get out of bed, I lay still for a few moments and repeat the following mantra,

"I align my power with the power of the Universe. I align my power with the power of the Universe."

And I imagine — and actually *feel* — my body merging with the

Universe. Yeah, I know it sounds weird but it's true and again, it *works*! I feel the boundaries of my physical body dissolve or merge with the space, i.e. the Universe, around me. This isn't my idea. It's not a tactic or maneuver I somehow created or that I have any jurisdiction over. It's just the truth. It's what life is beyond the physical limitations we erroneously place on it. And it's what life can be beyond the limitations your alcoholic husband has tragically placed on you.

Your world becomes very small and insular when you are married to an alcoholic. I remember I had a friend who was married to a doctor. Like any doctor, he spent his fair share of hours in the emergency room. Whenever I would let my then-young children do something particularly "dangerous" (like use "real" scissors — not "safety" scissors) she would caution against it. I just laughed at her caution and she admitted she had been influenced by her husband's constant admonishments over her letting their own children do "dangerous" things. (Like no safety scissors. Oh, the perils...) He himself had become jaded and lost perspective as a result of working in emergency rooms. To him, it must have seemed like children were "always" cutting themselves. He didn't really take the time to think about all the thousands (hundreds of thousands?) of young children who used scissors on a daily basis and never passed through the doors of an emergency room.

Something similar can happen to you when you spend all your time in the alcoholic marriage with an alcoholic husband. You lose perspective on how big and bold, bright and beautiful and powerful life, and you, are! You're not in this alone. It's not for me to define anyone's God or sacred deity. But I will take on the task of gently reminding you that there is a power, force, source, energy, light, love —.pick a moniker — that is greater than us and yet is us. Living with an alcoholic is like getting knocked to the ground and being pummeled with rocks, sticks and debris for so long that you forget you have legs to get up and run with.

The Universe (God, power, force, source, energy, etc., etc.) is your legs! Remind yourself the Universe is here! Reconnect with It. Partner up with It. Don't take on this creating-the-life-of-your-dreams thing alone.

You know (KNOW!) how horribly destructive and debilitating an alcoholic partner can be. And sure, it'd be a whole hell of a lot nicer to have the right partner in the form of a reasonably mentally healthy human being. But you and me, we didn't get that. Not right now anyway. So you need to turn to something different. You can call it prayer. You can call it re-connecting. You can call it aligning with the power of the Universe, as I have. It really doesn't make much difference what word or phrase you use. What makes the difference is that you take a few moments everyday to remind yourself that you are far bigger than the smallness of life in the alcoholic marriage.

.

LESSON #7

Move toward the Positive —
Not Away from the Negative

*The answer to any adversity is courageously moving
forward with faith.*
Edmond Mbiaka

Let me clue you in on a little secret:

It's not just us wives of alcoholics who risk standing idle as life
whips by.

Many, many (many) others, without nary an alcoholic in sight
I dare say, lose their dreams, their passions, their lives to the slow
erosion of time.

And whether you're married to an alcoholic or just the general
nature of life threatens your spirit, the problem is most of us become
trapped in the mire of trying to move *away* from the negative.

We think constantly of what we *don't* want.

We don't want to be fat.

We don't want to be in debt.

We don't want to stay at our present job.

And though it may seem counterintuitive, the fact is negative
consequences are not particularly powerful in motivating or changing
the human psyche. After all, how motivated is the alcoholic to
change? The consequences of compulsive drinking are about as
negative as one can get and yet wives and addiction experts alike
know the negative ramifications of compulsive drinking have little
impact on an alcoholic's ability or even willingness to change.

As the wife of an alcoholic, you probably spend a lot (A LOT!) of time thinking about how you just ("just?") want to GET AWAY from your alcoholic husband, his drinking, his behavior and the myriad of problems it all creates. Unforutnately, this puts you the untenable mindset of focusing on moving away from the problem, i.e. the negative.

A far more productive, healthier, not to mention just plain old more enjoyable, way to create change in yourself and your life is to focus on where you want to go, rather than on what you want to run away from.

I used to ride horses. Back in that life I had where I actually did things. When you are jumping horses, as you approach the jump you must look ten feet *ahead or past the jump*. And you never, ever look down to the ground!

That's right.

You don't look at where you are.

You certainly don't look at where you *don't* want to be, aka the ground.

You must look at where you want to go. The place at which you'd like to arrive, as one, you and the horse together.

It's easy to get wrapped up in looking only right in front of yourself — or staring at the (metaphoric) ground — when you are married to an alcoholic. After all, there is so much to continually draw your gaze there. But you have to resist. You have to retrain your brain to spend its time and energy looking to the horizon, to where you want to go. Because when you don't, when all you think about is how much you don't want to be where you are, ironically and tragically, that's exactly where you stay.

PART III

Creating Order

(Amongst the Ordered Chaos of Your Life)

You must have chaos within you in order to give birth to a dancing star.
Nietzsche

LESSON #1

Defining "Ordered" Chaos

You are not falling apart.
You are falling in place.

If I told you your life is filled with emotional, physical, spiritual and mental chaos as a result of being married to an alcoholic, I doubt you'd be surprised.

But what if I told you there is actually an *order* to the chaos?

What if I told you that your chaotic days of racing to work, raising the kids, taking care of the house and yes, managing your alcoholic marriage actually do have a rhythm to them? You may say,

"WHAT? I WISH!"

"Maybe your life has this 'ordered chaos' but did you see me this morning? There's nothing 'ordered' about my life. It's just pure chaos."

No, your life is quite ordered.

For your kids.

Your boss.

Your husband.

Even your pets.

What is pure chaos is your mental state. Your internal being. That's where all the chaos resides. Your mind is juggling 20 things at once.

You're feeding the dog while thinking about needing to wash your son's baseball uniform, get your daughter to a friend's house and what will you feed everyone for dinner.

You're putting dinner in the oven while thinking about getting your son's baseball uniform in the dryer while calculating what time you need to drop your daughter off in order to get your son to his game on time.

You're watching his game while thinking about picking up your daughter, getting home so the kids can do their homework and putting another load of wash in.

You set your kids up with their homework while you put that load of wash in so you can then go clean the kitchen as you answer homework questions the kids shout at you.

No one, not your husband, not your kids, not your dog ever feel like life skips a beat.

Except for those periodic times when you lose your mind over a soda bottle left on the coffee table or a wet towel dropped on the bathroom floor. For you to pick up. *Again!* You lose it. You scream. You yell. You threaten. You feel the weight of your alcoholic marriage bearing down on you as you rage beyond what would seem "normal." And then you go into your bedroom or lock yourself in the bathroom or hide in the back yard so that you might bury you head in your hands and cry. You hate your life, you hate your marriage, you hate your circumstances and worse of all, you hate who you have become.

Meanwhile...

Your family is just doing what everyone in your family normally does.

Ordered.

Chaos.

LESSON #2

Start by Getting Up in the Morning

Make each day your masterpiece.
John Wooden

I debated where to put this lesson.

Is this a lesson about creating order in your life or is it about creating movement toward your dreams?

Ultimately I decided it's more about creating order because before you can move toward your dreams, you have to stop, or at least minimize, the hemorrhaging of your soul's energy.

For many, many years there was nothing good or productive, likable or positive about my morning routine. I would actually set my alarm 60 minutes ahead of when I had to get up. I needed an entire HOUR of the snooze alarm before I could will myself out of bed. And once I was up, I certainly didn't have any sort of organized, productive routine. I was lucky if I actually took a shower and changed out of the yoga pants that had been my by-default pajama pants the night before — which had probably been the pants I wore all day the day before as well.

Clearly this was not a productive way to start my day. And I might still be floundering around with the bedtime + yoga pants = pajama pants = morning snooze button + day's attire if I hadn't happened upon a book called "The Miracle Morning" by Hal Elrod.

Hal Elrod "died" twice after being struck by a drunk driver. (And no, the irony is not lost on me.) When he got out of the hospital, he was faced with the daunting task of putting himself and his life back together again. Lucky for him, so to speak, he was also armed with the sort of deep and profound perspective one gains from surviving a virtually un-survivable accident. This is when he realized that the right morning routine could, indeed, literally change his life.

Elrod's idea is simple but powerful:

Start your day with direction and intent. He gives his morning routine/recommendation the acronym SAVERS.

Silence.

Affirmation.

Visualization.

Exercise.

Read.

Scribe.

You can find other authors, bloggers and sages on the Internet echoing the same sentiment. If you want to compare some of the different ideas and approaches for starting your day, that would hardly be a bad thing. Initially, I tried to follow Erod's prescription exactly but over time, I found I had more success tweeking his advice and ideas to better fit my life and temperment. The important thing (as with most advice for life) is not that you follow Erod's or anyone else's formula exactly: the important thing is that you incorporate the wisdom and power of a focused morning practice into your life in a way that works for you and creates success for you.

That said, it still took me a good solid year to fully implement my own morning routine into my life, starting with making my morning-me time non-negotiable.

I don't have to tell you this...

But I will.

Being married to an alcoholic is an energy-draining way of life.

If your alcoholic household is anything like mine — and good chance it is at least highly similar — you have to do everything around the house.

And I do mean EVERYTHING!!

Not a fork gets washed, not a piece of scrap paper gets picked up,

not a dust bunny gets swept if I don't do it. And so while the idea of
having a productive morning *sounds* good, it's another thing to drag
yourself out of bed each morning with the intention, expectation and
responsibility of actually following through.

Implementing a morning routine can feel like...

One...

More...

Thing!

(Or in the case of Elrod's book, seven more things.)

That you are responsible for.

Bed is your haven.

Sleep your reprieve.

Once you are up, you hit the the floor running.

And so who wants to get up *early*, even if it is for the supposed
good and benefit of your own life?

And you may even *want* to but wanting to and being able to are
two very different beasts.

No matter how right or productive, beneficial, promising or
even life-changing something may be, when you are married to an
alcoholic, is is *extremely difficult to think of placing one! More! Demand
on your already-depleted energy supply.*

So while I love Hal Elrod's book...

And while I would highly recommend working to implement
SAVERS or another purposeful morning routine into your life, if that
seems too much for you right now, here's what I suggest you do first:

Start by...

Just...

Getting...

Up...

A little earlier each day.

And by getting up, I mean getting up at the same time every
morning. A time that gives you at least a few minutes to sit quietly.
Early enough so you aren't rushing the kids or cursing the clock. Get

up at a time where you can simply be and breath and not feel like the world is crashing down on you before the day has even begun.

As they say, you have to crawl before you walk, walk before you run. I literally started by just getting up at 6 am every morning. No snooze alarm. No setting the alarm for 5 am. No different time on different mornings. Every morning. 6 am. I didn't really do much at first though I held myself to a firm no Internet or social media rule. I played around with the SAVERS until one morning I thought,

"Why don't I take a walk?"

Next thing I knew there I was, ME!, walking at 6 am!

And I liked it! (Not always but most of the time.)

Implementing a morning routine isn't suppose to be a punishment.

It isn't meant to be another thing you require of yourself but fail at — and then beat yourself up for.

This is *for* you.

Really.

A gift.

Something you are giving to yourself.

Maybe at first you do nothing more than sit quietly in your living room.

Or talk a long, hot, uninterupted bath or shower.

The vital thing is that you commit yourself to getting up early enough each morning so that your own personal morning routine and rituals can develop. Don't make the mistake of expecting yourself to be immediately capable of implementing a "perfect" morning routine. Training your mind is no different than training any other muscle in your body. If you wanted to start a weight-lifting program, you'd hardly expect to start off with 100 pound weights on day one. If you wanted to run a marathon, you wouldn't lace up your shoes and head out to run 15 miles on your first training day. It's easy to recognize how any sort of physical endeavor requires a gradual, systematic approach to training and yet we expect mental training to be instantaneous.

You are TIRED!!

And yes, a thousand times yes, establishing a new, productive morning routine WILL create more energy for you — *in the long run* — but first you have to work with the (lack of) energy you have!

So get up.

Maybe take your shower early.

Maybe journal.

Maybe go for a walk.

The trick is to initially not place too many demands on your morning rise. If journaling comes easy to you, then yes, journal. If the idea of a walk sounds heavenly, yes go for a morning walk. But if you aren't yet comfortable with writing or if you'd rather pull out your own toenails with rusty pliers than go for a walk first thing in the morning, don't try to use such things as motivation for training yourself to get out of bed in the morning. It'd be like a dangling a rotten carrot in front of a donkey's nose — and then expecting her to pull her cart in pursuit of it. It wouldn't work with a donkey and it won't work with the human psyche. Be gentle with yourself. Give yourself time. Start by simply getting up in the morning. You'll figure out what your own delicious carrots are in due course.

LESSON #3

Start a Meditation Practice

So what is a good meditator? One who meditates.
Allan Lokos

Meditation is one of those things that we hear about and we know we "should" do it and we may even want to do it but it sounds so hard and mysterious. And how could we possibly know how to *meditate*? Wouldn't we have to take like a class or something?

Well, I am all for taking classes, learning from masters and expanding our experiences through the wisdom of others *but...*

Guess what?

Meditation is really nothing more than taking the time to quiet your mind and become fully present in your body and the moment. It can be for a minute, it can be for five minutes. It can be ten, 20, 30 minutes or more. Tibetan monks can meditate for hours and actually slow their brain waves down.

But you're not a Tibetan monk and you don't need that degree of meditation in order to reap the vast myriad of benefits meditation has to offer. What you do need is the willingness to commit to a daily meditation practice and to hold its place in your life as sacred and consecrate. (i.e. it's not something you do just whenever you happen to have the chance.)

So how exactly do you meditate?

It's pretty simply actually. Your brain already knows what to do. It's just getting You out of the way to let it do it.

Find a quiet place, obviously, where you don't have to fear being interrupted. I like to meditate early in the morning when I can be confident my kids will be sleeping for a few hours more. I actually find the *fear* of being interrupted more distracting than actually being interrupted. It's difficult to be fully present in your mind, body and the moment if you're worried that at any moment, someone could come bursting in and proclaim wiht shock and horror:

"WHAT ARE YOU DOING MOM?! YOU'RE SO WEIRD!"

So the first, most crucial step since without it you can't go any further, is to find the time and place. I actually meditate in a hot bath though that may not be appealing to all. Just find the place that works for you, though not your bed — for very obvious reasons. I like to play "meditation" music that I find on YouTube though complete silence works as well. You can put pretty much put any variation of "music to meditate by" or "Buddhist meditation music" and even "Tibetan wind chimes" in the search bar and get a satisfactory list of choices to choose from.

Before you settle in, use the bathroom, get a drink, turn off your phone, put the dog out, etc., etc. All the sorts of things that are suddenly going to demand that you be up and moving when you are trying to be still and quiet.

Then set a timer. I set it for 30 minutes. No, I do not usually meditate for 30 minutes but 30 minutes is long enough where I won't be interrupted by the timer but short enough where I won't be distracted with thoughts of, "God! Is this ever going to end?" Or "When the hell is the timer going to ding?"

Sit down (do not lay down. GUR-AN-TEE you will fall asleep!) and get comfortable. No, you don't have to cross your legs and hold your arms and hands awkwardly out to the side. Just sit comfortably. Turn on the music, close your eyes and think about nothing. When random thoughts like "I forgot to plunge the toilet" try to occupy your mind, don't attempt to stop them. Don't try to "not" have them. Just let them sort of float on by without any reaction or engagement by you.

One trick for controlling your thoughts without trying to control

them is to start at the top of head and focus your attention there.
Continue progressing down your body, focusing your attention on
your forehead, your eyes, your nose, your ears, etc., etc. I visualize
this sort of blue energy-light moving down my body, kind of engulfing
me like the giant slime monster in a B-horror movie. Only nicer.
Calmer. More peaceful.

And there you have it.

My basic, rudimentary meditation explanation and process.
Of course meditation is like any art form; you can spend years
developing and strengthening your practice. But it's important not to
let yourself get intimidated or scared off by the notion that "basic" or
"rudimentary" is bad or not enough. Meditation is about taking time
to quiet your mind and be present in your body in the moment. You
don't need anything special — be it instruction, music or a bamboo
mat. Of course, if you do find yourself really drawn to the practice
of meditation, there is nothing wrong with exploring it further.
Just don't think you "have to" in order to reap the benefits of a daily
meditation practice.

LESSON #4

De-Clutter — Kinda!

Your home should rise up to meet you.
Oprah

What on Earth, you may be thinking, does the clutter in my house have to do with my marriage to an alcoholic and how I prepare to leave him (even if I'm not ready to leave him)?

Well, if you have no clutter in your house and/or what clutter there is doesn't bother you a rat's whisker, then de-cluttering (kind a!) really has nothing to do with your alcoholic marriage and how you prepare to leave it. You are free to skip ahead. *But* if there is clutter and it does bother you, then you probably understand immediately why I mention it here now.

Clutter is a big topic for the world these days — alcoholic marriage or not.

Have you ever been to the "Container Store?" An entire store devoted to... *containers!*

There are organizational experts who will come into your home and teach you how to organize your crap — for a $150 an hour!

And type "books on organizing" into Amazon and you will not be disappointed. It seems a good majority of the world is spiritually suffocating under the weight of all the crap we own! So why am I including a lesson on de-cluttering in a book about how to (prepare to) leave your alcoholic husband?

Because clutter is both an energy-drain and a deflector. It will draw you in and use your energy and deflect your time away from the real goal of creating the life of your dreams.

There is way too much crap in my house.

It seems to assault me on a daily basis.

I spend hours everyday "cleaning" and "organizing" and yet my house is never clean or organized. What's even worse is I don't even know why I care so deeply!! I have never been a "neat freak." The woman and mother I was PAH (pre-alcoholic husband) would have *never* chosen cleaning over doing something with her friends, family or children. And yet now I find myself longing for my husband and children to leave for a weekend.

So I can CLEAN!

If you find yourself obsessing over *stuff* rather than living your life, consider that it may have little to do with the *stuff* and a lot to do with feeling out of control in your life.

Do you know why alcoholics are so mean and controlling?

Because they feel out of control internally.

Alcoholism is a tireless, wicked and merciless taskmaster. It swirls about in its victim's head continually creating chaos and discord. The alcoholic is in constant conflict with his alcoholism. He's either indulging it, denying it or denying he's indulging it. And so he goes outside himself, looking to control his environment since he can't control his internal state of being.

Ironically, as the wife of an alcoholic, you are in danger of doing something very similar. You can't control your husband or his drinking or his behavior or the downward spiraling of your marriage so you become fixated on controlling your environment.

It took me years to realize I was so desperately trying to control the physical state of my home because I felt I had no control over the emotional, spiritual and mental state of my being. Of course, with an alcoholic husband and growing children, it was pretty much impossible (ok, it was completely impossible) to ever achieve that sense of "control." But that didn't stop me from trying.

And wasting precious time, energy and money in the effort.

Hope springs eternal I guess and so I bought bins, boxes and books all designed to help me organize my life. And while I don't want to say these books were useless or wrong, they did seem "useless" and "wrong" in the alcoholic household. For example, one book I bought was the best-selling book by Marie Kondo "The Life-Changing Magic of Tidying Up." In it she advises you to purge your clothing by dumping the contents of all your dressers and closets into one big pile on your bed and then systematically going through it.

Ostensiably in one sitting.

Do you have any idea what would happen if I dumped all my clothing into a big pile on my bed?

I know exactly what would happen.

I would have the chance to purge a t-shirt or two, maybe a stray sock in one sitting but that would maybe be about all. The pile would become the new forever-home for everything in it, gradually creeping and spreading across my room like some sort of giant, gelatinouse clothes-amobea monster.

You and me, the wives of alcoholics, we don't have time for such. There is too much pulling on us, demanding of us, draining us for us to have that kind of time and mental energy to devote to organizing.

I was stuck in a proverbial Catch 22:

I didn't have the energy to address the clutter in my house but the more I lived in the clutter, the more it drained my energy. And the more I tried to contain the clutter, the more I became frustrated and angry. And the more frustranted and angry I became, the more I kept trying to fix the very thing I couldn't fix. The very thing that was draining my energy, making me frustrated and angry.

A rat on wheel had nothing on me.

Of course, a neater house would not have necessarily made it any easier to have my husband call me a fucking bitch or watch him drink all weekend. But your physical space is a very powerful force in your life. Your home is not an inanimate "object" or benign "entity" and the state of it is one more complication in life with an alcoholic husband.

I had to do something but the somethings I kept reading about were not going to work in my life.

So I came up with my own something.

I decided I was going to throw out or put in a donation bag *ten things a day.* I would go through my house and pick up ten things. And *every! Single! Thing counted!* I had read somewhere that "like items" should only count as one. Not for me. Big or little, one of one or one of many, every individual item counted as one. And that included caps or tops that had been separated from their "bottoms!" Additionally, once I discarded ten things, that was it. I crossed "de-cluttering" off my day's to-do list.

I know it sounds over-simplified and indeed, at its conception, I wasn't sure this approach would work. But no other approach, philosophy or methodology had worked for me so what did I have to lose? My need wasn't so much to have my house and stuff de-cluttered quickly (though I would have welcomed that!). It was to give myself some sense of control over my physical space while also freeing my mind from the constant energy-drain of thinking about, worrying about, toiling at cleaning and organizing my house.

And it worked.

Of course not right away or all at once. It took several months for me to really see and feel a difference in the pure level of stuff in my house. But the process was cathartic and powerful. The alcoholic affects everything in your home, from the emotional and spiritual to the mental and physical. When you're trying to somehow mitigate or contain these affects, it can be easy to get sucked into the idea that you have to fix everything all at once. That's about as effective — and as impossible — as trying to herd cats. But when you break it down, when you do *something*, even if it feels tiny in comparison to the largeness of the alcoholic, and you do it consistently, you not only create great change outside yourself but you create great change within yourself.

Where you really need it.

PART IV
Preperation and Movement

When I was five years old, my mother always told me
happiness was the key to life.
When I went to school, they asked me what I wanted to
be when I grew up.
I wrote down "happy."
They said I didn't understand the assignment and I told them they
didn't understand life.
John Lennon

LESSON #1

Decide What You Want Your Life to Be

I did then what I knew how to do.
Now that I know better, I do better.
Maya Angelou

With my formater's deadline nipping at my heels like a hungry jackle, I reached this part of the book in my editing efforts. The original lesson in this place was "Determine What You Want Your Leaving To Look Like." I had written honestly and sincerely about what had been my struggle with staying focused and committed to the effort to prepare to leave my alcoholic marriage and how I overcame that. The problem is I had written those words over four years ago. When I was in a different place as both the wife of an alcoholic and in my growth as a human being. Now, no matter how I tried to tell myself to simply tidy up the awkward sentences, fix the missed typos and get the revised manuscript in on time, I just couldn't endorse those ideas now. There had been too great a shift within me.

For so long, all I wanted was my own house!

God! I just wanted my own house!

It's all I thought about.

When my husband would be cursing at the dog or yelling over some random infraction, I'd think...

I just want my own house.

When I would drop my kids' off at their friends' pleasant, neat, orderly houses, I'd think...

God! I want my own house!

When the enormity of all the half-finished projects and needed repairs or maintenance of our house assaulted and overwhelmed me, it was as though my body physically ached for its own house.

And every night, when I would go to bed and the room was freezing and my husband's blasted white-noise fan was whirling in my ears, a desperation for my own house would rise up from within me and threaten to consume me.

I just wanted my own house!

A nice house!

An organized house!

I house I could be proud of and feel good about.

A house I could have guests visit without a weekend of cleaning first.

A house that was warm and inviting and comfortably — physically as well as emotionally.

And so because "all" I wanted was my own house, like any good, card-carrying metaphysics following, hippy-loving new age-embracing individual, I focused on manifesting said "own house."

I circled future dates on a planner and wrote in big, bold, confident letters: CLOSE ON MY NEW HOUSE.

I bought kitchen towels and measuring cups for my new house.

I drove through neighborhoods and visualized myself arriving home.

I bought moving boxes and packed stuff up, with cryptic labeling that I knew meant "for my new house."

I adjusted my expectations — as I had described in the original lesson called "Determine What Your Leaving Looks Like" — so that my new-house manifestation goal felt more in align with who I saw myself to be.

And every night, when I would lie down in our bedroom that felt like a meat locker and sounded like an airplane hangar, I would visualized myself in my own warm, quiet bedroom with a big giant fluffy comforter and a couple cats sleeping at my side. (My husband doesn't want pets in the bedroom and I will admit that is not the most outrageous of requirements.)

I worked that manifesting machinery to the fullest.

So why no house "instantly?"

Well, basic human rookie mistake #1:

I was trying to fix my inside being by changing my outside environment.

I was a vibrational, energy-wise hot mess!

I was angry. I was bitter. I was hostile. I was resentful and regretful.

I thought, ("knew") if I could just somehow get this unaligned, vibrationally spastic, discontinuous ball of energy known as Me into a beautiful new house, all would be ok. Better than ok.

Perfect and charming and peaceful.

From there, in the sanctity of my own home, during quiet early mornings, with the sun peaking in the window of my idyllic breakfast nook, a cup of herbal tea at hand and my laptop before me on a gorgeous, handcrafted farmhouse table, I would fix all that pesky negativity and anger and resentment that had taken up residence within me.

The problem is neither life nor the much-toted tool called "manifestation" works that way.

I was angry and cluttered and disorganized and chaotic and so what I manifested (aka my house) was angry and cluttered and disorganized and chaotic.

Don't worry about what your potential future leaving may or may not look like or even if it will or will not happen.

Worry about what you want your life to look like.

Now.

Preparing to have the choice to leave isn't about preparing your leaving strategy, as I erroneously believed initially. It's about preparing your life so you can one day implement a leaving strategy should you so desire. I spent too long focusing on the specifics of leaving when I should have been focusing on the specifics of creating the life I envisioned for myself — alcoholic husband or no alcoholic husband.

LESSON #2

So Who Do You Want to Be?

If you want light to come into your life, you need to stand where it is shining.
Guy Finley

I've always known myself to be a writer and artist and I was fortunate in my life to have parents who recognized and encouraged my talents and dreams. And yet, it still took me 50 years to get around to actually applying myself to the pursuit of these dreams and the realization of my gifts. Maybe it wouldn't have taken me quite so long had I not married an alcoholic. (Or maybe the Universe used my alcoholic husband as the pressure I needed to become my own diamond.) Either way, I grew up with some pretty aware and supportive parents and I still got derailed big time.

So what if you didn't have supportive parents?

What if you've never had anyone recognize and acknowledge your special talents, gifts and attributes?

What if you were put on this treadmill called "life," set at "reality" at a young age and now you have no idea who you are or what your dreams may be?

First, I am going to challenge you and say you do know.

Deep down inside.

Where no one else can hear.

Thoughts whisper to you in the middle of the night or while you're sitting in traffic or when you are bored out of your mind at your cubicle enclosed desk.

I'm not talking about the fantasy chatter about buying a lottery ticket and winning $10,000,000 or writing a book that becomes an instant million dollar best seller. I'm talking about that little tiny ember within you, fighting for you to fan it, longing to burst into flame.

Maybe it's a writer.

Maybe it's an artist.

But maybe it's a baker or chef.

Maybe it's a florist.

Maybe it's owning your own cleaning service. I have a friend who LOVES to clean.

Not all dreams have to be of an esoteric nature — artist, dancer, actor, writer, etc. I have a family member who started a concrete business. He loves pouring concrete! But whether it's artist or construction worker, singer or pastry chef, there's something inside of you that is only of you.

If you've never been allowed to see yourself as someone more than your parent's child or your children's mother or your alcoholic husband's wife or a boss's employee, now is the time. If you had that knowledge of who you are beyond all those identities the world heaps on us but lost it in the chaos of an alcoholic household, now is the time.

To decide who you really want to be.

Who you came to be.

What is your purpose for your visit to Earth?

What is your greatest, secret-est desire for yourself and your life? That thing that you dare share with maybe no one, maybe only a single closest confidant. None of us — not a single, solitary soul of all the billions of souls here on Earth, came to be "just" anything. And certainly not just the wife of an alcoholic.

The alcoholic husband and marriage will erode you of all you once knew yourself to be. And if you never got a chance to know who you really are? Well, then, the alcoholic marriage will strip mine your soul.

I had a pretty strong sense of who I was and still I felt myself losing myself to the toxicity, trauma and dysfunction of an alcoholic marriage. I tried to save myself by focusing on getting out. Buying my own house. Now I see what I should have been focusing on was fortifying as well as developing the Me I knew myself to be. Figure out who You are. Nurture and develop Her. Encourage Her to come fully into Her own being.

Despite being married to an alcoholic.

LESSON #3

Don't Focus on Money

God never gives you a dream that matches your budget.
He's not checking your bank account.
He's checking your faith.
Pinterest

Money, money, money, money, money, money, money, money, money, money...

Money.

Money.

Money.

Money.

MONEY!

In Part II, "The Metaphysical," I suggested you ask the Universe for a money-reality shift. That's part one of what is essentially a two part process in freeing yourself from your erroneous beliefs about the scarcity of money while also creating financial abundance for yourself. The part two is this:

Don't focus on money.

When my finances were tied to my husband's, it was quite maddening because all he worried about, thought about, obsessed about and yelled about was...

How'd you guess?

Money!

It didn't matter if I said I wanted to take the kids across town for frozen yogurt or across the country to Disney World. I'd get the same response.

"We don't have ANY MONEY!"

It was quite literally *impossible* to have any (ANY!!) sort of conversation with him about our finances. The very minute I dared broach the subject, he'd start yelling that all I did was spend "all" the money and there was "no use" discussing anything financial with me and nothing was "ever" going to change and things would "never" improve for us financially. It was clearly toxic on so many levels but when I stepped back and really examined our interactions and *his* attitude, I realized the biggest problem with his money issues was that they were creating *my* money issues. Whenever I would get overwhelmed and desperate about my life and marriage (and that happened on a pretty regular basis) my own inner dialogue would go something like this:

I have to get out! God I have to get out!

I don't have any money!

How am I going to leave when I have no money?

I need to make money?

How am I ever going to make "enough" money?

Oh God, if only I had money...

Money, or more specifically, a working belief in and an obsession with the scarcity of money kept me stuck far longer than a true lack of money. It wasn't "money" I needed to let go of as much as it was my ideas and beliefs that money is scarce and "making money" is hard and that I'd never have enough anyway.

Money is such an emotionally charged subject and entitiy for so many people but really money is just energy. It's energy in a physical form that we as humans have agreed upon. People don't feel unworthy of having the energy of health or the energy of food or the energy of friendship but for some reason, money trips so many of us up.

Trust that money is simply another form of energy that you are welcome to enjoy in abundance.

Let go of the idea that in order to bring money into your life, you have to obsess over bringing money into your life.

Refuse to subscribe to the idea that money is holding you back in life and if you "just" had "enough" money, everything would be ok.

Stop believing any of this is even about money anyway.

Yes, in order to one day have the *option* of leaving or staying in your alcoholic marriage, you need money. As in your own money. Enough money. But that doesn't mean your focus should be on "making" money. Have you ever heard the saying, "do what you love and the money will follow?"

I think it's more accurate to say,

"Be the very best You you can be and the money will follow."

LESSON #4

The Movement Requirement

*If what you're doing is not moving you toward your goals,
then it's moving you away from your goals.*
Brian Tracy

Ok, so you've adjusted, realigned and changed your feelings, your beliefs and your expectations regarding your husband and your marriage.

You've ventured — either full on or with little tiptoes but nonetheless you've ventured — into the realm of the metaphysical.

You've worked hard to calm the chaos of your life, implemented your own version of a "miracle morning" and started meditating as best you can.

You've even allowed me to convince you — or at least you're considering the idea — that the best way to create future options for yourself is by focusing your efforts on becoming the best version of yourself you can be right now. All while ignoring the almighty and alluring dollar.

So now what?

Sit back, and wait for the Universe to deliver your new and improved, alcoholic-husband proof life via Amazon?

Yeah, not so much.

The truth is that nothing — and I mean absolutely nothing — I have written or has ever been written about changing your life, realizing your dreams, finding your bliss and living life to its fullest and grandest potential suggests or implies that you don't have to actually *physically work, act and move* to make it all happen.

Yep, that's right.

Nothing will ever happen if you don't ACT.

You thought changing your feelings about your marriage, believing in reality shifts and ignoring the need for money was hard?

That stuff is nothing compared to having to bring yourself to physically move toward your dreams.

This is where the rubber meets the road, as they say.

The pee or get off the pot...

Fish or cut bait...

Nose to the grindstone...

Get some skin in the game.

Etc., etc., etc.

But what exactly does it mean to "act?" How do you move toward your dreams and goals?

Well, it's really very simple.

In fact, it is so *simple,* as to be somewhat complicated.

You physically move toward your goals and creating the life of your dreams by, drum roll please...

Making physical movements toward your goals and dream life.

Yeah, I know...

Seems a little... obvious?

Except most of us often get tripped up because we misunderstand what "doing" really is.

We think that "doing" means doing great BIG specific things to create a great BIG specific path toward a great BIG specific goal.

For example, if you want to lose weight, you join Weight Watchers or Jenny Craig or Nana's Weight Loss Camp and you eat exactly "right" everyday and you exercise everyday and you lose two pounds a week. Every ounce of your effort and energy to lose weight goes toward doing the sort of things people say you must do in order to lose weight — planning meals, counting calories/carbs/"points," going to the gym every single day, etc.

If you want a better job, then you spend every waking second scouring ads, searching the Internet, contacting your contacts. You beef up your resume and you apply, apply, apply until finally you score that coveted new job.

If you want a more organized house, you read books, throw stuff out and feng shui the hell out of everything from the backyard patio to the family pooch.

Whether it's your weight, your job, your house, your marriage or any other endeavor, you treat each like it's a separate entity in your life that needs to be pursued separately and individually.

But what if it's more complicated than that and yet easier?

What if life isn't a bunch of separate boxes — job, weight, home, health, spiritual, mental — that need to be filled individually? What if there is *overlap*?! What if any movement or progress you make in one area of your life actually *assists* or *benefits* all areas of your life?!

Well, that's exactly how it works!!

The Universe isn't keeping a check list or spread sheet on what action you make toward which goal. (Nor is your psyche but more on that later.) The Universe, and the human condition as it were, craves and loves and responds to *movement*!

Any!

Movement!

The Universe is ready!

It's there, on the edge of its metaphysical seat, *just waiting* for you to do *something* so it can start working its magic! Think of it as you're the brawn and the Universe is the coincidence-producing, serendipity-creating, happy-accident making brains of this operation called Your Life. But it can't produce "coincidences" or "happy accidents" or any "serendipitous encounters" if you're not making room for such in your life.

When I was about 25 years old, I decided I wanted to take horseback riding lessons. The way it worked at the barn I chose, probably all barns, is they assign you a horse based on your riding level. When you are a beginning rider, truth be told, you're not really "riding" the horse as much as the horse is taking you for a ride. A rider communicates her desires to the horse through her hand and leg movements. A beginner's hands and legs, however, are all wobbly and wonky, moving this way and that, sending a barrage of very mixed messages to the horse without even realizing it. If a beginner were to get on a horse that truly needed to be ridden — directed, guided and communicated with — it would be a disaster for both rider and horse. The horse would receive all the unintentional, conflicting and contradictory messages of the beginning rider's hands and legs and try to respond. The rider would be dragged around the ring by a seemingly annoying though earnest horse.

So to save both (wo)man and beast, the beginner rider gets a plug of a horse, as they say, that needs nothing from the rider. The old school horse that has done these lessons 100's of times so no matter what the novice rider may inadvertently be telling the animal, it simply goes through the motions. Walk, trot, turn, stop. Walk again. The horse has been doing the same thing in the same lesson for so long, it barely has to pay attention.

Well, the Universe kind of gets like that in regards to your life. It just kind of plods along on some sort of metaphysical autopilot. You can't really blame it. You're like the riding instructor telling the same tired old horse to do the same tired old drills lesson after lesson after lesson. Just instead of communicating "walk, trot, stop, turn, walk again..." you tell the Universe — over and over again —

I'm fat.

I'm overwhelmed.

I'm defeated.

I'm tired, broken, lethargic.

I hate my house, my pets, my life and even myself.

And so, just like the aging school horse trudging through yet another lesson with yet another beginner on its back, the Universe may show up for you everyday, but it's just doing the same old thing in the same old way you've told it to do time and time (and time!) again.

It's like the Universe says,

"OK. You're fat and miserable and married to an alcoholic. You're overwhelmed. You have no energy. You hate your life. You're angry and hurt, resentful and despondent. You're hopeless. I got this…"

And it's not simply that you put this metaphysical message out there for the Universe to receive.

You *act* this way too!

And when you feel and act hopeless, defeated, broken and overwhelmed, all the Universe can really do is support you in living a hopeless, defeated, broken and overwhelming life. But if and when you start acting differently? When you begin to move in a different direction? When you change the energy you are projecting out into the world?

The Universe not only notices but it responds.

Right away!

It bolts awake from its metaphysical slumber and shouts,

"WOW!! Now she has given me something to work with!"

And it's not just the Universe that has been laying dormant. Your psyche has slipped into its own groggy state of being. It goes through its own set of tired, old habituated actions so that it might best get through the days while trying to protect and numb you to the realities of life with an alcoholic. I had a friend who's son was diagonosed "ADD" but he hated and mostly refused to take the prescribed medication. (I say good for him but that's a whole different book.) He said the problem with the medication was it dulled everything about him — not just his tendency to be distracted or his inability to concentrate fully. It's sort of like this when you are married to an alcoholic. You can't dull your emotions and feelings when it comes to his compulsive drinking and accompanying behavior but remain highly engaged and passionate about the rest of your life. Not without a conscious and consorted effort.

And small actions everyday.

I felt stuck for a long, long, long, long…LONG!! time as a result of my marriage.

Everyday (EVERY! DAY!) I dreamed and planned and hoped — God I woke up with hope — that the day before me would be *The* Day I began to change my life.

And every night (EVERY! NIGHT!) I went to bed feeling the same sense of failure and defeat. The end of another day where I had yelled at my kids too much and done too little that would help create the life I longed for.

It wasn't until I finally...

Finally, finally, finally, finally...F-I-N-A-L-L-Y understood that I was not going to change my life and achieve my dreams "all at once." That all the big, big, BIG ideas I had for my life actually required a lot of little, little, LITTLE bits of effort.

Every.

Single.

Day.

It's like deciding you want to run a marathon...

And expecting yourself to go out and run ten miles on your first day of training.

Life is gradual.

No matter how much Amazon wants you to believe you can achieve gratification instantly with its drone delivery service and pick-up lockers, this basic tenet of life will always remain the same.

Everything takes time.

That's the "bad" news.

The good news is all movement, any movement, will create change within you and the Universe.

Any movement!

Don't think in terms of what you need to do specifically right now. Think in terms of what you can do *differently*.

You can start your day with a walk.

You can begin journaling.

You can "make" (as in allow) time for yourself sit down with each of your children for 15 minutes and simply be present with them.

You could find a church, if that aligns with your beliefs.

You can find an organization to volunteer with! That probably sounds like about one of The CRAZIEST things! How the hell will you have the time and energy to volunteer somewhere when you barely have the time and energy to get through each day? Well, let me tell you. In the midst of all the chaos in my life, I began volunteering with a hospice organization. Surprisingly, I found giving to other people (in a way that wasn't doing laundry, making dinner and driving mom's taxi) actually renewed me, rather than further draining me.

I can't say it enough:

As the wives of alcoholics, we become stuck.

Emotionally, mentally, spiritually and physically.

We especially get stuck in the idea that in order to change our lives and improve our own mental state, we need to make big, all encompassing movements in whatever particular area of life we want to change. Luckily this is not so. When you strive to create change and growth in one area of your life, you will be creating change and growth in all areas of your life.

LESSON #5

Focus

Lack of direction, not lack of time, is the problem.
We all have twenty-four hour days.
Zig Ziglar

Focus.

Simple word.

Easy concept.

Complicated and hard to do.

Life is busy these days.

For everyone.

But when you're married to an alcoholic, life is busy *and* and you can feel like you are carrying an extra 180 pounds (give or take depending on your husband) of dead weight on your back.

My husband would be so hurt to read that.

And I'm sorry.

I really am.

But that's pretty much how life with an alcoholic feels.

Everywhere I turn (EVERY!! WHERE!!) there is something to be done:

The laundry, the cleaning, the kids, the cooking, the grocery shopping, the pets. Then there are the repairs and the routine maintenance-turned-repair projects around the house. And don't forget a few dream projects — like painting the living room that hasn't been painted in over ten years.

It's like my house is full of hundreds of neon signs all flashing: FIX ME!

CLEAN ME!

PICK UP ME!

PAINT ME!

REPLACE ME!

FINISH ME!

I feel like I've been herding cats for the past 15 years. I don't finish anything: I just continually get different things at different times to a semi-tolerable state. If the laundry is basically done (off the floor, washed and in the dryer) you can bet the kitchen is a mess. If the kitchen is clean, the bathroom is probably disgusting. And if I manage to get any outside yard work done? For sure the inside of my house looks like a tornado went through. And then there are all the half-finished projects that seem to taunt me from the corners where they have been shoved in my attempt to make them go away.

No one can do "everything" and as the wife of an alcoholic, you can do even less of everything.

So you have to focus.

You have to shut things out.

Make them go away. Maybe not physically but certainly mentally.

Accept — for now anyway — there are things that need to be "good enough" as they are.

I rescued a set of four gorgeous dining room chairs from the side of the road. The chairs themselves were in great condition but the cushions needed to be replaced. I planned on doing just that.

Over five years ago!!!

It was hard (at first!) to put those chairs back on the curb to be re-rescued but it was also very liberating. I had to admit to myself that those chairs were doing nothing to help move me toward my big goal — creating financial independence and autonomy — and were actually taking away from my goal. You may not think looking at four chairs I had planned to repair (over five years ago) took a toll on my mental energy but it did. Every time I spied those chairs, or worse, had to move or navigate around them, it was like opening a spigot and letting my energy drain out. Maybe not a lot. Maybe more of a slow drip but a drip nonetheless.

This sort of stuff adds up.

If it was just one set of chairs, so to speak, it might be ok but in the alcoholic household, there are LOTS of "chairs." And so if you want to create the life of your dreams, you have to decide which chairs to focus on and which ones to ignore. Or even stick back on the curb.

There were so many (SO MANY!) projects to be completed in my house and I so (SO!!) wanted a nice, comfortable home but I finally realized:

I could either direct my energy toward creating the home I wanted in the house I was living in (and not a bad or wrong choice) or I could devote my energy to creating the financial abundance and independence I needed to buy my own dream home. For me, I chose the latter. I wanted my own house! I wanted it SO BADLY!! And so I had to accept that there were many things I had to turn a blind eye to.

How do you know what to ignore in your life and what to focus on?

Ask yourself this simple question:

Does directing my attention, energy and efforts on this particular task help me move toward my goals or does it take me further away from them?

PART V
Living Your Life

Life is a great big canvas and you should throw all the paint on it you can.
Danny Kaye

LESSON #1

Live Your Life Where It Is

Learn to enjoy every moment of your life. Be happy now.
Don't wait for something outside of yourself to
make you happy in the future.
Think how precious is the time you have to spend,
whether it's at work or with your family.
Every minute should be enjoyed and savored.
Earl Nightingale

If your life is miserable, why would you want to live it where it it?

You hate where your life is.

It's at the corner of hopeless and hopelessness.

The Avenues of the Broken.

Exhaustion Boulevard.

You don't want to live your life where it is.

You want to get on a train and travel as far away as quickly as you can.

And yet, the great irony, paradox, contradiction, trick, plot twist and cruelty of any transformation is this:

In order to change what you hate into something you love, you have to love and embrace and honor the very thing you hate as if you loved it.

Huh?

In other words,

If you want to create a life you love from the life you hate, you have to love the life you hate.

Clear as mud now?

For far too many years of my life, the sun didn't set on a single

day — not a single day — where I hadn't spent some time during that
day — sometimes it was just a moment, sometimes it was the entire
day, but regardless, not a single day passed where I didn't curse, hiss,
lament or declare,

I hate my FUCKING life!

Sometimes the declaration was an exasperated whisper under my
breath; sometimes it was a full-blown, yelling-out-loud, profanity-
laced proclamation; sometimes it was just a fleeting thought in my
head: sometimes it was not fleeting in the least, but no matter how
the sentiment expressed itself and with what intensity and duration,
it was a constant expression I gave life and merit to.

In fact, it was the very foundation I so earnestly tried to build a
new life on. My new life. My new life that I would love. That's about as
good an idea as having kindergardeners pour the foundation for the
house you want to build.

Unfortunately, this is where the chaos and toxicity, the regret and
resentment of living with an alcoholic husband takes you. It destroys
your sanity, you peace, you joy and, most tragically, your sense of self.
Alcoholism is an insatiable beast that gnaws on your soul and then
uses the splinters as a toothpick to pick at the bits of you stuck in its
filthy fangs.

And so when you finally feel ready and able to change that...

When you're prepared to stand up and fight for the life you long for...

When you hear yourself say — *I'm not living like this one minute
longer* - with a conviction that as of yet had been absent...

It can be easy and understandable to lose sight of the fact that while
you work to change your life, you still need to live the life you have.

Remember the sitcom "MASH?" Or perhaps I should say, "there
once was this sitcom called "MASH," as I am really dating myself here.

It was a hughly popular show that aired in the 70's and 80's. It was
about a "mobile army surgical hospital, aka MASH, that was situated
on the front line of the Korean War. The whole show was predicated
on juxtaposing the business of living with the horrors of war and

serving on the front line. Believe it or not, it was a comedy.

It showed the men and women of "MASH" living life best they could while bombs dropped all around them and the horribly wounded were rushed into make-shift surgical wards.

They formed friendships. They fell in love. They fell out of love. They had affairs. They had hobbies. They questioned their place in the Universe and wondered as to the purpose of life.

They even laughed and had fun.

In other words, they lived life.

Of course, they also longed for, wished and waited for the day when the horror would be over — whether for everyone or just themselves — and they would go home.

This is life with an alcoholic husband.

It's not hyperbole to say that when you are living in an alcoholic household, you are living in a war zone. The alcoholic husband offers his own threats of bombing by way of his erratic moods, explosive anger, compulsive drinking and accompanying behavior. You become accustomed to mitigating, tip-toeing, ducking, dodging and avoiding his artillery. But at what cost?

Most often at the cost of your own life and soul. That's why it's not enough to simply prepare your life so you will one day have the choice to stay or leave: you have to protect and live the very life you have right now. Even though it's on the front line of an alcoholic's war.

"And exactly how am I supposed to DO THAT?" You may ask.

It might seem like the answer lies in taking on some great challenge outside yourself. Like training for a marathon. Or walking five miles everyday. Maybe you're thinking you should save to go on safari in Africa. Perhaps learn to rock climb, scuba dive or skydive.

Certainly quite worthy endeavors that could be a boatload of fun (except the marathon. How could running for 26 miles be even remotely FUN?!) but it's not where you need to, or even necessarily should, begin.

I spent a long, long, long time thinking I had to change the physical properties of me and my life in order to start living my life "where it was" but that is exactly what "living your life where it is" is *not*.

So what does "lving your life where it is" really mean?

It means recognizing that even if your life, your marriage, your home, your husband your everything-about-life is not what you desire, even if it's something you detest, your life right now still has merit and value. And now still *counts*.

Time isn't on hold while you are miserable.

Your life isn't paused because you are unhappy.

The sands of time are running through the hour glass whether you're pursuing your life's passion or cursing your daily existence.

Living your life where it is is about waking up every morning and finding — or creating — a way to enjoy your life just as it is. Living your life where it is is finding joy in places, i.e. your life, where you didn't think there was joy to be found. Your soul isn't dying due to lack of safaris or marathons or adrenaline-charged endeavors like skydiving. Your soul is dying because your alcoholic husband drains the pleasure out of everyday living. He leaches the happiness out of an easy morning on the back deck with a good cup of coffee. He drains the joy out of gardening. He destroys the simple pleasure of reading a book. Or baking cookies with your kids. Taking a walk around the block.

There was so much I used to do. Maybe it wasn't the stuff that glossy print ads or television commercials are made of but it was stuff that made my life whole and complete. I used to...

Get up early in the morning and take my dog to a field to run and exercise.

Take "night time" walks with my kids.

Go to the library and check out books I *actually* read.

I used to knit.

Play board games with my kids after dinner.

Bake with my kids.

I even went hiking on the weekends with my kids.

There were so many (SO! MANY!) simple, inexpensive things I did right in my own home or just outside my front door, so to speak, that made me feel alive and passionate and like I was living life — not just letting life happen to me.

What sort of things did you *once do?* What simple pleasures made you feel like you were living true to who you came to be? Put the safaris or European vacation on hold. Let the rocks, the ocean depths and the marathons wait. Forget about starting that "million dollar" company.

For now.

You can't withstand the bombing in an alcoholic marriage by having dreams that feel far away. No matter how earnestly you work toward them. I'm not saying don't have dreams. Have dreams. Have the big, fantastical, beyond-your-wildest-dreams dreams. But don't confuse these dreams, or even the pursuit of these dreams, as the only way — as a mandate even — to enjoy your life on a daily basis. When my father was dying from cancer, more than once he heard,

"Why don't you take a big trip?"

It confused, confounded and sometimes angered him. He usually just shrugged it off but he confided in me,

"Why would I want to take a big trip? I'll still have cancer. If these are my last days, I want to spend them with my family, in my home, being around the people and pets and things I love and doing the things I've done for the past 25 years."

My dad wanted to work in his wood shop.

In the evening, he wanted to watch tv while eating ice cream with me like we had for so very many years.

And he definitely wanted to sleep in his own bed, with a view of the backyard where he raised his children, with the love of his life, my mother, by his side.

You don't need some sort of grand endeavor or adventure to start living your life again. What you need is to ask yourself,

"What was my life about before the Beast of Alcoholism hijacked it? What little things filled my days and brought me pleasure before his drinking began consuming me and everything around me?"

The Beast robs you of your life. Bit by bit. Day after day. But you can also take your life *back* bit by bit, day by day. It's easy and natural to feel completely powerlessness against the wrath of someone's else's compulsive drinking.

And indeed, you are powerless against *his* drinking.

But don't exasperate that powerlessness by remaining powerless in your own life. Don't give away the power you do have by clinging to the erroneous (and destructive) idea that the only solution for taking back your life lies in pursuing some great, overwhelming goal or endeavor.

You have to court your life again.

Fall back in love with your life.

Cultivate a love affair between you and your life.

Everything is eroded when you live with an alcoholic.

I looked up one day and realized I had no "clothes" to speak of. Oh, I had yoga pants and t-shirts — which are quite handy when you wear the same thing out into your day as you wore to bed the night before. How telling is it about your mental and emotional state when you've all but given up on your physical presentation?

I didn't take my dog for walks anymore. I used to drive around and look for fields that she could run and play in and yet, here I was, doing little more than letting her in and out the back door.

I all but stopped doing things with my children. Of course, they are growing up and my relationships with them changing, but still, it seems I was so worried about "cleaning" and "organizing" my house until one day, I had forgotten the things we used to enjoy together.

I couldn't have told you the last book I read for pleasure. One more thing, a piece of me, something I had enjoyed, lost to the chaos of an alcoholic household.

These are the places you need to turn to to find your life again. To renew your passion for your own living. The fact is, the longer we live in the chaos of an alcoholic marriage, the more our minds become *addicted* to the emotions of that marriage. Dr. Joe Dispenza is a neuroscientist who has written many books on the subject of neuroplasity. The idea that the human brain can be molded and changed. Our minds will actually become addicted to negative thought patterns and the release of the couresponding neurotrasmitters. We will *look* for ways to ignite the anger just as the addict looks for his next hit.

You have become physiologically and chemically trapped by your husband's drinking. Your responses and reactions are habituated reactions that are now wired into your own brain chemistry. You and me, we're no different than the alcoholic in that sense. Our behavior changes the wiring of our brains until the wiring of our brains changes our behavior. But little things really will start rewiring your brain. It wakes the brain up. Requires it to think again rather than continue on autopilot. It's not going to be comfortable getting out of bed and going for a walk when you've spent the last ten, 15 years hiding from life for a long as you can every morning. But this discomfort is exactly what you, your brain and your life need.

Another great way to jolt your brain out of it's wired-complacency is take a class with your local rec department, at a community college or specialty store. (For example, yarn stores will often offer knitting classes.) The brain can't concentrate on learning a new skill *and* your husband's drinking at the same time. While you're in the class and at home practicing your new craft, your brain will be forced to rewire itself.

Go to a movie by yourself. I *love* going to movies by myself! It may feel awkward at first but what a delicious reprieve from the alcoholic marriage. And again, it's an action you can take that sends the message to you and your brain,

"I'm worth it. My life is worth it. I am more than an alcoholic's wife."

Do something that shakes you up a bit. Makes you feel a little nervous or fills you with some trepidation. It doesn't have to be jumping out of an airplane or scaling a mountain peak. It just has to be something that rattles the complacency that has settled on your life, your brain, your daily routine. Push yourself to move beyond simply enduring another free trip around the sun.

Life with an alcoholic husband will easily imprison you in a cell of despondency and hopelessness, but you really do hold your own key.

LESSON #2

Trust the Process

*To have faith is to trust yourself to the water. When you swim you
don't grab hold of the water, because you will sink and drown.
Instead you relax and float.*
Alan Watts

I read or saw or heard once — don't really remember who or when or
where — that "goals are dreams with a deadline." The un-remembered
source went on to say that without time frames and deadlines, dreams
are powerless and pointless.

I couldn't disagree more.

I think the statement is faulty no matter what your dream or
particular situation may be but it becomes particularly faulty and
problematic when you're living in the dynamic of the alcoholic marriage.

For the majority of us, creating the ability to have the choice to
leave our marriage will take a fair amount of time. To add an arbitrary
"deadline" to the endeavor, to put the pressure of time on yourself will
not give you a sense of empowerment and direction. It will not give
you motivation. Rather, it runs the risk of exasperating your sense
of helplessness and the seemingly forever-ness of your situation.
Telling yourself "just" five more years when the Beast of Alcoholism
is rearing its ugly head on a daily basis will not magically infuse you
with a newfound sense of passion and enthusiasm for living. No, a
clock ticking — be it literal or metaphorical — will most likely just
leave you feeling the same sense of defeat and despondency that you
already feel on a daily basis.

"Five more years of THIS?!" Your soul will scream.

Whether you try to be "realistic" and assign a reasonable time frame to your efforts or you try to push yourself to achieve what can feel like the un-achievable in a short time, you really are setting yourself up for failure. Instead, you should strive to create new routines, rituals and habits in your life *that support where you want you life to go and then...*

Know that in this mysterious ethos called Life on Earth, there is a power — be it God, The Universe, Energy or "The Force" — that is conspiring to bring all your efforts to fruition.

Trust the process.

Think of the gardener.

She prepares the soil and plants her seeds. But then, does she lament that nothing is ever going to grow? Does she dig up the seeds everyday to see if they have sprouted? Does she demand the seeds do their magic according to random marks on a calendar?

No, of course not.

She prepares the soil, plants her seeds, provides the necessary food, water and care and then lets the magic happen. She leaves the seeds to their own because she knows that all that needs to be happening is indeed happening, albeit beneath the soil and out of her view.

Changing your life is exactly like this.

If it sounds simple, (though simple and easy are not the same thing) that's because it is.

Simple when you compare it to living with an alcoholic, anyway.

Life in the alcoholic marriage is about surviving — emotionally, mentally, spiritually and maybe even physically. You're not building or creating the life you want. You're simply enduring the life you have as you make it from one day to the next. So when someone like me says "all" you have to do in order have the life of your dreams is create new but different daily rituals, habits and focuses," as my kids would say,

"That's crazy talk."

But it's true.

The real way — the only way actually — to change your life in big ways is to change your life in little tiny ways on a daily basis. Life with an alcoholic is overwhelming enough without heaping more pressure onto yourself by way of deadlines and time frames. Instead, concentrate on creating little microcosms of change on a daily basis. Plant the seeds of your life, tend to them on a daily basis but trust them. Leave them to let the magic happen. Deep in the soil, out of sight from you, but happening nonetheless.

LESSON #3

This S**T Is Hard

If you would only recognize that life is hard, things would be so much easier for you.
Louis D. Brandeis

Ok, so the night before I wrote this very lesson, my husband had one of his "fucking this-fucking that" screaming fits. I have no idea why I am still surprised by these. Perhaps even more surprising is that even after nearly ten years of such episodes, they still leave me emotionally stunned and debilitated. I feel mentally paralyzed and completely unable to work toward the goals and dreams I so earnestly want and believe in. I guess I get lulled into a false sense of security when several weeks go by without him screaming his vulgarities at me. (You "might be" married to an alcoholic if the bar is set so low that "not screaming" is the best you can hope for.) I was merrily going along writing this tome, believing and trusting, feeling hopeful and positive when...

BAM!

Out of left field, he verbally sucker punched me when I brought up money. (It's always money for him.)

"ALL YOU DO IS FUCKING SPEND MONEY! YOU JUST WANT TO FUCKING SPEND MONEY. I'M WORKING MY ASS OFF AND WHAT DO I HAVE? NOTHING BECAUSE YOU SPEND EVERY FUCKING DIME I MAKE."

Nice, I know.

Four hours later, my kids are fighting and I grab my daughter by the arm and I scream at her,

"I'm so GODDAMN SICK of this BULLSHIT."

That's what I screamed at my daughter.

That's what I screamed at my daughter because I live with a husband who screams at me.

I am by no means proud of my actions.

More like sickened by my actions.

And I don't tell you this to in any way to legitimize how I act in response to how I am treated.

I tell you this to remind you that breaking free of the beast that binds our husbands is hard.

Very hard.

It takes sustained and consistent commitment to changing your life in little ways on a daily basis so that your life will change in big ways on a long term basis. And that "sustained" and "consistent" commitment can be very hard when living with an alcoholic. It can feel like you're pushing a boulder uphill and for every two feet you go forward...

It rolls back one.

That's the bad news.

The *good news* is that while yes, it can feel like this, it *only feels like this in the beginning!!*

I started and stopped my efforts at change only to start and stop, start and stop...start and stop over and over and over again for many years. But I never gave up and neither should you. Because one day all my efforts paid off. One day I got myself out of that damn starting gate and galloping around the track! Give yourself six months.

REALLY!

Not ever single physical dream and change will necessarily manifest itself in six months time but there will be a monumental shift in you emotionally, mentally and spiritually.

And that can go a long, long way in sustaining you while the physical changes come to fruition

So don't give up.

Don't stop requiring more of yourself.
But don't beat yourself up either.
It's hard pushing a boulder up a hill.
Especially when someone is sitting on it.
But the crest may be closer than you realize.

LESSON #4

Change Your Internal Dialogue

Don't believe everything you think.
Dr. Wayne Dyer

Can you imagine going to your kid's baseball or soccer game and yelling,

"You guys are terrible! There's no way you'll ever beat this team!"

Can you hear yourself telling a friend who is going through a difficult time,

"Your life sucks. There's nothing you can do about it. It's never going to change."

How about telling a friend with a serious or terminal illness,

"I think you may as well give up because you're going to die from this."

Of course not.

You would never utter a single word even closely resembling these sentiments and yet...

It's the kind of stuff you probably say to yourself every single day!

Everyday, and I mean EVERY! DAY! I would be screaming in my own head,

"I HATE MY FUCKING LIFE!"

"I HATE THIS HOUSE!"

"I HATE THESE GODDAMN ANIMALS!"

"I HATE MYSELF!"

Every.

Day.

And it was a real, visceral and palatable hatred. It wasn't simply thoughts in my head. I felt it down to the very fiber and core of my being.

I **HATED** my life, myself, my house and nearly everything in and about my life.

And I reminded myself of and reaffirmed this hatred over and over again on a daily basis.

You can't say that kind of stuff to yourself and then expect yourself to somehow rise up and create and live the life of your dreams. It will never, ever, ever....*EVER* work! As corny and awkward as it may sound, you have to start saying nice things, positive things, loving things, sweet things to yourself! It's not going to come naturally. Not at first anyway. You've been living in the environment of an alcoholic household for so long that it's now your "natural" response to react to your life with words and thoughts of hatred and despair. Why wouldn't you think about how much you hate the chaos, the fighting, the drunkenness, the vacancy, the pain of living with an alcoholic husband when that is what you're living with everyday?

Like any effort at change, changing your internal dialog is paradoxically simply but difficult. In order to change your internal dialog, all you have to do is...

Change your internal dialog.

When you walk into your house where not a dirty dish has been cleaned, not a project finish, not a wet towel picked up off the floor, you simply tell yourself,

"I love my house. I am so grateful for a home."

When your husband is staggering around drunk, either begging to argue with you or make love to you — because let's be honest, both are equally revolting - you just say to yourself,

"I love me. I am so glad to be me."

Kids screaming and fighting and acting out from their own internal chaos and confusion? Yep, just remind yourself how much you cherish and love them.

Now, you're not going to believe or feel any of this love or gratitude or harmony at first. No, you're head is going to be screaming,

"ARE YOU CRAZY?! I DO NOT LOVE THIS!"

But you can't give into *those* thoughts. You can't legitimize or validate *those* feelings. Every time your psyche tries to throw in a negative, hateful or ugly thought, you shoot it down with something decidedly over-the-top sweet and positive!

Our dog.

Oh I HATED our dog!

She was out-of-control, untrained. 80 pounds of thrashing, barking power barreling in on me when I walked in the door.

God, I hated her. Yes, I knew her behavior was our fault and yes I knew she was just one more manifestation of the chaos of an alcoholic household but that didn't make it any easier when I was trying to get in the house with an armful of groceries.

"GET DOWN!"

"GET AWAY!"

"GO ON!"

I'd be yelling at her while in my head is sceaming,

"I HATE THIS DOG! I FUCKING HATE THIS DOG!"

Well, you can imagine how far that went in motivating me to embrace my dog and actually work with her. I knew I needed to work on training her. (No one else was going to do it.) I even told myself I was "going to" but it seemed I just never got around to it. Instead, it was the daily barrage in my head of,

"I HATE THIS DOG!"

Then one day, I decided I would do nothing more than stop saying I hated her. I told myself I would say I love her when I walked in the door. When she was jumping on me and barking at me and knocking everything within a tail-wagging-distance down, I would hug her and pet on her and think kind thoughts. I didn't have to take her for walks or train her or do anything more than simply change "I hate her" into "I love her." After all, she didn't jump on me *any less* when I was screaming,

"I HATE THIS DOG!"

Once I changed my inner dialog with the dog, everything began to change externally. No, she didn't instantly train herself but I calmed down. I felt less anger and angst upon walking into my own home. I reconnected with her. And yes, eventually I found the energy and time to actually train her.

You just can't go around cursing and damning yourself and your life while simultaneously hoping to repair and reclaim yourself and your life. You have to say nice things to yourself about yourself and your life. You have to encourage yourself and build yourself up with your thoughts and words, not tear yourself down. You have to replace words like hate, never, horrible and can't with words like love, grateful, happy and can.

And you have to do this before you necessarily believe it, Even — especially - before the physical realities of your life warrant it. It's (flawed) human nature to want what's outside of you — your relationships, your home, your job, your children, your dog even — to change *first* in order to change what's within you. It will never, ever, ever work in that order. How, why would I have started walking my dog, working with my dog, making an effort to train my dog when I was constantly screaming at her, and reinforcing in my own mind, "I HATE YOU!" Who wants to do anything for or with something they hate? It sounds simple. It sounds corny. Maybe it even sounds too easy but changing the running dialogue *inside* your head is one of the quickest ways to change what's *outside* your head.

LESSON #5

It's All a Head Game

Life is 10% what happens to you and 90% how you react to it.
Charles R. Swindoll

Years ago I saw a print ad for a watch. I don't remember what brand
of watch — so maybe not a very good ad — but I do vividly remember
the tag line. There was a picture of a competitive swimmer in a pool
and the ad read,

"Life Is A Head Game."

I don't know why this ad made such an impact on me but it did.
And this was before I began living life as the wife of an alcoholic. If I
saw the ad today, I'd want to tell the copywriter,

"If you think ordinary life is a head game, try life with an
alcoholic. It's a head game on steroids."

Essentially everything about being married to an alcoholic — from
simply enduring life to trying to create a life where you thrive and
flourish - is one big head game. There is no way (NO WAY!) anything
is happening or changing for you and your life without a lot (A LOT!)
of mental preparation, rewiring, and a determined, focused effort at
changing yourself internally.

In other works, you have a lot of work to do.

To state, restate and understate the obvious: the alcoholic
marriage really does a number on your psyche. It erodes and corrodes
everything that once made you you. Everything you probably ever
valued and enjoyed about your unique self is nibbled on, gnawed on,
macerated and devoured by The Beast. The foundation of You, your

own personal infrastructure, is being destroyed.

And yet, often most of us try to fix ourselves and our lives without addressing this decay.

I know I did.

I'd wake up every morning *determined* to *not* let the state of my marriage and the crumbling decay of my soul affect me. I was not going to snap at my kids or yell at the dog or be pissed off about the disarray of my house. I was going to be happy and energized and enjoy my life despite my husband and The Beast who were clawing at my being.

Most days that attitude and hope didn't last past mid-day. Some days not past my morning trip to the bathroom.

Something needed to change.

And that's when I realized it was me, as in me internally.

I was trying to fix what was broken with what was broken: I had to fix the broken before I could fix the broken.

(And since you're married to an alcoholic, I know that makes perfect sense.)

There is little doubt your thought patterns and beliefs have been hijacked by The Beast of Alcoholism. The spiritual, mental and emotional death that befalls you as the wife of an alcoholic is so subtle, so gradual, so insidious but cancerous that you can miss how deeply and profoundly you are being affected. And so before you can amass your fortune, start your million dollar company, write your best seller, paint your masterpiece, create your viral-presence on the Internet, stop eating half a dozen doughnut for breakfast every morning or "just" create a life of choice and purpose, you have to change what's going on inside your own head.

Nothing is going to change in your life accidentally. Simply *wanting* your life to be different will do very little to actually creating a different life. You have to start in your head. You have to make a conscious effort to change the flurry of thought patterns, tired, habituated thinking and knee-jerk reactions that are ricocheting about in there.

Life is indeed a head game.

And life with an alcoholic an allout mental war.

AND FINALLY…

Consider the Gift of Alcoholism

All the adversity I've had in my life, all my troubles
and obstacles, have strengthened me.
You may not realize it when it happens,
but a kick in the teeth may be the best thing in the world for you.
Walt Disney

We come to my final offering in regards to how to create the life of your dreams, while creating the future of your choosing while living the life you have right now.

Wow!

That's a tall order for any writer or book.

No wonder I was afraid to hit the final "publish" button.

But I did and I hope you have found at least a few words, ideas or suggestions that guide, inspire, motivate, focus and/or shake you up enough to propel you toward a more deliberate and conscious way of living. The final idea I would like to challenge you with is this:

Consider seeing his drinking as a gift.

"WHAT?" You may want to scream?!

"A GIFT?! What kind of GIFT would that be? His drinking does nothing but TAKE! I thought a gift was suppose to *give!*"

Well, I won't disagree.

Being married to an alcoholic destroyed, diluted and polluted EVERY…SINGLE…THING I thought my life, my marriage, my family and even myself would be. It stole my past, my present and was poised to steal my future. It turned my kids against one another (we are all slowly healing now). It turned me against myself. It feels as though it has made me cry more (and I hate to quantify grief) than the deaths of my father and mother combined. Being married to an alcoholic rotted my soul in a way I couldn't have imagined possible had I not experienced it myself. It made me hate everything about myself and my life.

And yet it turned out to be one of the greatest gifts I ever received.

Being married to an alcoholic forced me to do things I may have only ever dreamed of doing.

It made me focus my craft as a writer and *actually* write books rather than *planning* to write books.

It made me confront my biases and preconceived notions about money in order to create my own financial security and freedom.

It forced me to grow spiritually and emotionally. It demanded that I did the work so that I — not anyone else - rescued my soul from the savage fangs of the Beast of alcoholism.

Would I have preferred this work and personal growth come via an emotionally present, mentally healthy, loving and supportive husband? Would I have rather reached my dreams by way of a marriage that lifted me up and empowered me? Did I spend many days and nights longing for a husband who was my equal partner, biggest fan and soft place to land? Of course I did.

When I got married, I dreamed of the all the same things any woman dreams of as she walks down the aisle. I imagined (expected) a life that my husband and I would greet together, with mutual respect, admiration and love. I thought we would face the struggles and embrace the joys as a united front. Together we would raise our children, clean up dog puke, lament about the cost of braces and bemoan the speed at which our children were growing up. We would lay in bed at night and dream of the beach cottage where our grandchildren would come to spend the summers with us. I certainly didn't even remotely entertain the idea of,

"Hey, how about my husband pushes me to the edge of craziness and when I am just about to plummet to my emotional and mental death, *I* pull myself up. *I* save myself. *I* create the life of my dreams *in spite of* my marriage, not *because of* my marriage."

No one wants a gift that makes you work. It's like being given a vacuum cleaner or a dishwasher. We want the sort of gifts that come wrapped in pretty paper or in that signature-blue Tiffany box. Maybe a car in the driveway on a snowy Christmas morning with a giant red bow. (Yeah, just to be clear, I don't know ANYONE who has ever gotten that — alcoholic husband or not.) We want gifts that sparkle and shine and make us deliriously happy when we receive them.

We don't want a gift that makes us cry and hate, mourn and grieve.

We don't want a gift that makes us challenge our own limits and boundaries. And then requires us to push ourselves beyond them. We don't want a diamond that comes in the form of a hunk of coal.

And yet, that's exactly the kind of gift an alcoholic husband is. It's a sad, mad, hideously ugly gift that no one would ever choose at the office Christmas party. It's the present you're stuck with at the end of the white elephant gift exchange. It's the gag gift you stuff in your purse, vowing to dump it in the first trash can you come to.

The gift of alcoholism is everything that can be bad or go wrong or be disappointing about the lovely idea of gift-giving.

And yet...

Like any and all adversities in life, you have the choice and the power to make it the greatest gift you've ever received. I hate to mix my metaphors but eventually it comes down to this:

Your husband's drinking will either be the anchor that pulls you to the bottom of the sea to drown or the wings that allow you to take flight.

Unfurl your wings.

RESOURCES

One of the best ways to move beyond living life with an alcoholic is to stop approaching life from the base of living life with an alcoholic. The fact is that at the end of the day, no matter what challenge, obstacle, heartbreak or impediment life has put in your way, you are still responsible for how you respond. Following are some of the books, both fiction and non-fiction, that were helpful in my journey to move beyond "living life with an alcoholic" to *living life!*

"The Miracle Morning"
by Hal Elrod
This is the book that set me on the path to having a focused, deliberate morning routine. It's shocking how simple but powerful a morning routine can be.

"You Can Heal Your Life"
by Louise Hay
Also, her website louisehay.com has many other books and resources Louise Hay is kind of like the grandmother of the whole metaphysical movement. A visionary before her time, she published "You Can Heal Your Life" in 1984, when the idea (fact) that our thoughts and emotions are connected to our physical well being and existence had not yet really made its way into mainstream thinking.

"Your Erroneous Zones"
by Dr. Wayne Dyer
Dr. Dyer passed away in 2015 but he too, like Louise Hay, was an early

pioneer of bringing the metaphysical to the general public. He has many, many books ("Change Your Thoughts, Change Your Life: Living The Wisdom of the Tao," "The Power of Intention," and "Being In Balance: 9 Principles for Creating Habits that Match Your Desires" are just a few others) that teach us that we are infinitely more than what may be happening *outside* ourselves and that the power to change ultimately lies *within* ourselves.

"Infinite Possibilities: The Art of Living Your Dreams"
and *"Manifesting Change: It Couldn't Be Easier"*
by Mike Dooley
His website is tut.com
I like Dr. Dyer's books and I've enjoyed watching many of his specials on PBS. He was like a wise, scholarly grandfather encouraging you to be the very best You you can be. Well, Mike Dooley is another writer and motivational speaker who speaks on the metaphysical and the power we all carry within ourselves but where Dr. Dyer is more grandfather-ly, Mike Dooley is like the fun, wacky uncle. His writing and presentations (I was fortunate enough to be able to attend one of his day-long workshops a few years back.) are ever bit as powerful as Dr. Dyer's. His books do tend to be a little shorter (definitely a plus in our chaotic lives) than Dr. Dyer's and he has a more "modern" vibe to him. He's not "better" than Dr. Dyer but he does have a decidedly different style that may resonate with you in a different way.

"The Little Book of Mindfulness: 10 Minutes A Day To Less Stress,
More Peace"
by Patrizia Collard
I love this book because it exemplifies the power of making small changes on a daily basis. We all want great big sweeping change in our lives but this book shows you that the real way to big change is through little changes performed on a consistent basis.

"The Four Agreements"
by Don Miquel Ruiz
This book is based on Toltec philosophy, an ancient philosophy
that believes wisdom, good, power and divinity resides in us all. It
basically says watch how you use the spoken work (though I would
say the thought-word as well); don't take anything personally (what
wife of an alcoholic doesn't need to develop *that* mental muscle);
don't make assumptions and always do your best. Really, the kind of
things we heard in elementary school (or should have) but may have
forgotten along the trail of life.

"You Are A Badass: How To Stop Doubting Yourself and Start Living An
Awesome Life"
by Jen Sincero
This book is fun, it's irreverent and it takes a refreshing approach
to the "self-help" genre. With Dr. Dyer as the grandfather and Mike
Dooley the wacky uncle, Jen Sincero will round out your library nicely
as the tell-it-like-it-is, get-in-your-face, supportive-to-the-very-end-
friend who gives good advice without being too sappy or allowing any
of your excuses.

"Jonathan Livingston Seagull"
by Richard Bach
What can I say about this classic? No list of "how to live a more
conscious life" would be complete without this fable about a seagull
who wants "more" from life than the daily gull-existence.

"The Alchemist"
by Paulo Coelho
I love this book. The book follows a young shepherd boy, Santiago,
as he pursues his "Personal Legend." Your "Personal Legend" is
that which you have always wanted to accomplish and what "all the
universe conspires in helping you to achieve." It's the metaphysical

meets fiction with the result being a story that is enjoyable to read as a work of fiction while also encouraging you to fulfill your own destiny. To strive for your own "Personal Legend."

CONTACT

Blog: WrenRWaters.com

Email: WrenRWaters@gmail.com

You were born with greatness.
You were born with wings.
You are not meant for crawling, so don't.
You have wings.
Learn to use them and fly.
Rumi

Made in the USA
Middletown, DE
30 September 2023

39821867R00102